Better Homes and Gardens®

WHITE CROCHET

First Edition. Second Printing, 1988.
Library of Congress Catalog Card Number: 87-63204
ISBN: 0-696-01630-3 (hardcover)
ISBN: 0-696-01631-1 (trade paperback)

BETTER HOMES AND GARDENS® BOOKS

Editor: Gerald M. Knox
Art Director: Ernest Shelton
Managing Editor: David A. Kirchner
Editorial Project Managers: James D. Blume,
    Marsha Jahns, Rosanne Weber Mattson

Crafts Editor: Joan Cravens
Senior Crafts Editors: Beverly Rivers,
    Sara Jane Treinen

Associate Art Directors: Neoma Thomas,
    Linda Ford Vermie, Randall Yontz
Assistant Art Directors: Lynda Haupert,
    Harijs Priekulis, Tom Wegner
Graphic Designers: Mary Schlueter Bendgen,
    Mike Burns, Brian Wignall
Art Production: Director, John Berg;
    Associate, Joe Heuer;
    Office Manager, Michaela Lester

President, Book Group: Jeramy Lanigan
Vice President, Retail Marketing: Jamie L. Martin
Vice President, Administrative Services: Rick Rundall

BETTER HOMES AND GARDENS® MAGAZINE
President, Magazine Group: James A. Autry
Editorial Director: Doris Eby
Editorial Services Director: Duane L. Gregg

MEREDITH CORPORATION OFFICERS
Chairman of the Executive Committee: E. T. Meredith III
Chairman of the Board: Robert A. Burnett
President: Jack D. Rehm

WHITE CROCHET
Editors: Joan Cravens, Sara Jane Treinen
Editorial Project Manager: James D. Blume
Graphic Designer: Linda Ford Vermie
Contributing Graphic Designer: Patricia Konecny
Electronic Text Processor: Paula Forest

Cover project: See page 23.

CONTENTS

SPECIAL TREASURES

ALL WHITE AND WONDERFUL

Romantic, elegant, fresh, lively—such are crochet designs stitched in the many varieties of white threads and yarns. Whether you love the look of old-fashioned lace, the grace of a snowy afghan, or the softness of a baby's sweater, you'll find projects aplenty in this chapter and those that follow.

Five crocheted flowers (primroses, star flowers, gloxinias, petunias, and cluster flowers) are tucked into the nosegay, *below.* Stitch each design in just a few rounds and add them to a bridal bouquet or other arrangement as a memento of a special day.

The filet-crochet banner, *opposite,* features an alphabet, epigram, and homey scene similar to those found on traditional cross-stitch samplers. The design measures 11¼ x18 inches.

Directions for designs in this section begin on page 12.

SPECIAL TREASURES

Edgings—wide or narrow, simply or intricately wrought—hold a special place in the hearts of many crocheters. With an edging, you can dress up the plainest of purchased or handmade presents, and transform a commonplace piece of fabric into an uncommonly pretty (and personal) accessory.

The tailored trim on the runner, *above,* is only 1¾ inches wide and features a stylized primrose stitched in filet crochet. Make the edging in one piece, mitering the corners and adjusting the design to fit any size cloth. (The runner

shown measures 8¼x52 inches, excluding the lace.)

The picket-fence design on the cloth, *opposite,* also can be worked to fit any size cloth. Here it's sewn to a 15x24-inch piece of embroidered linen (the perfect size for a pillow sham). Worked in Size 30 thread, the lace measures about four inches wide.

SPECIAL TREASURES

A five-petal flower forms the center of the small doily, *above*. Craft this design using Size 20 thread and single, double, treble, and double treble crochet stitches. Chain loops form the lacy, graceful background mesh. Diminutive fans, created with double treble crochet stitches and accented with picots, border this nine-inch-diameter doily.

(For each double treble crochet stitch, yarn over *three* times, then draw up a loop in the stitch. Wrap yarn over the hook and draw through two loops *four* times.)

Experienced stitchers will enjoy the challenge of creating the unusual 24-inch-diameter centerpiece, *opposite*. Six roses, each set into a brick-patterned background (made with chain-five blocks instead of the usual chain-two blocks), surround a center rose in this spectacular piece.

SPECIAL TREASURES

Edgings and doilies needn't always be used in conventional ways—sewn onto hems or set onto tables. *Opposite*, a circular edging threaded with bright ribbon stands out atop the lavish ruffle on a round pillow. And, *above*, two doilies shine on plump rectangular and eight-sided pillows.

Stitched in Size 20 thread, the lace edging, *opposite*, measures five inches at its widest points. Sew the edging onto a 13-inch circle of chintz and add a wide ruffle behind it for an eye-catching 22-inch-diameter pillow.

The filet-crochet rose pillow, *above*, measures about 11x13 inches without the ruffle when worked in Size 30 thread. The lily-of-the-valley design, worked in Knit-Cro-Sheen, is about 12 inches in diameter. Tack both of these pieces over plain fabrics that complement your color scheme, then trim with piping and wide print ruffles.

Row 4
Row 5

Row 95

Row 105
Row 106

Row 109

FILET HOUSE SAMPLER

☐ Open space (sp)
■ Filled block (bl)

'Bless This House' Filet Sampler

Shown on page 5.

Sampler is 11¼x18 inches.

MATERIALS
DMC Cordonet Special crochet cotton, Size 20 (174-yard ball): 3 balls of white
Size 10 steel crochet hook
13-inch-long, ¼-inch-diameter wood dowel
Cornstarch
Heavy cardboard, at least 14x20 inches
Waxed paper
Rustproof straight pins

Abbreviations: See page 78.
Gauge: 14 dc = 1 inch.

INSTRUCTIONS
Note: This sampler is worked differently from traditional filet-crochet projects. For this project, one open space is a dc followed by one ch-1. When working an open space over an open space in the previous row, dc in dc, ch 1, dc in next dc. When working an open space over a block, dc in dc, ch 1, sk dc, dc in next dc.

One block is a dc followed by one dc. When working a solid block over an open space in the previous row, dc in dc, dc in ch-1 sp, dc in next dc. When working a solid block over a solid block in the previous row, dc in 3 dc. Two solid blocks in a row equal 5 dc; three solid blocks equal 7 dc.

Work the first three rows following the instructions *below,* then begin to work from the chart, *opposite.* Since the sampler is worked from the top down, turn the chart upside down to make it easier to follow. Always read odd-numbered rows from right to left; read even-numbered rows from left to right.

Beginning at top, ch 164.

Row 1: Sc in second ch from hook and in each ch across; ch 5, turn—163 sc.

Row 2: Sk first sc, work dtr (yo hook 3 times) in second sc and in each sc across; ch 1, turn.

Row 3: Sc in first dtr and in each st across row, sc in top of turning-ch; ch 3, turn—163 sc.

Rows 4–5: Referring to chart, sk first st, dc in each st across row; ch 3, turn.

Row 6: Sk first dc, dc in next 4 dc; (ch 1, sk dc, dc in next dc) 77 times; dc in next 3 dc and top of turning ch; ch 3, turn—77 ch-1 open sp.

Rows 7–95: Work even from chart, working ch-3 turn at end of each row; do not ch-3 at end of Row 95.

Row 96: Sk first dc, sl st in next 2 dc, ch 3, dc in next 2 dc; work from chart; do not work in last 2 sts; ch 3, turn.

Rows 97–105: Follow chart, working decreases at the beg and ends of rows; fasten off.

Rows 106–109: Join thread and complete each point separately following chart. Fasten off.

FINISHING: Join thread at top left corner of sampler; work one row of reverse sc (work from left to right) across top; fasten off.

Join thread on one side; work one row of sl st evenly spaced along this side; rep on opposite side; fasten off.

STIFFENING: Mix 1 tablespoon of cornstarch in 2 cups of cold water and stir to dissolve. Cook until clear; let cool. Soak sampler in mixture. Wring sampler; roll in towel. Pin to cardboard covered with waxed paper; let dry overnight. Run dowel through dtr at top to hang.

Crocheted Flowers

Shown on page 4.

MATERIALS
DMC Cebelia crochet cotton, Size 10 (50-gram ball): 1 ball of white
Size 7 steel crochet hook
Florist's wire and floral tape
Pink stemmed-flower centers

Abbreviations: See page 78.

INSTRUCTIONS
See photo on page 14 for close-ups of flowers.

PRIMROSE (A): Beg at center, ch 5, join with sl st to form ring.

Rnd 1: Ch 3, work 2 dc in ring; (ch 3, work 3 dc in ring) 4 times; ch 3, join with sl st to top of beg ch-3—5 ch-3 lps.

Rnd 2: Ch 2, holding back last lp of each dc on hook, dc in next 2 dc, yo, draw through rem 3 lps on hook. Ch 3, * **holding back last lp of each trc, work 3 trc in next ch-3 lp; yo, draw through 4 lps on hook—trc-cl made.** Ch 3, **holding back last lp of each dc, work dc in each of next 3 dc, yo, draw through 4 lps on hook— dc-cl made.**

(Ch 3, work trc-cl in next ch-3 sp, ch 3, work dc-cl over next 3 dc) 3 times; ch 3, work trc-cl in next ch-3 sp, ch 3, join with sl st to top of first dc-cl.

Rnd 3: * Sl st in next ch-3 sp; ch 4, work trc-cl in same sp, ch 4, sl st in same sp; rep from * around; join with sl st to first ch of beg ch-4; fasten off.

STAR FLOWER (B): Beg in center, ch 5; do not join.

Rnd 1: **Holding back last lp of each trc on hook, work 3 trc in fifth ch from hook, yo, draw through 4 lps on hook—beg trc-cl made. Ch 4, holding back last lp of each trc on hook, work 4 trc in same ch as beg trc-cl, yo, draw through 5 lps on hook— trc-cl made.** (Ch 4, work trc-cl in same ch as first cl) 3 times; end ch 4, sl st to top of beg trc-cl.

Rnd 2: In *each* ch-4 lp around work **sc, hdc, 3 dc, ch 2, sl st in last dc made, 3 dc, hdc, and sc— petal with picot made.** Join with sl st to first sc; fasten off.

GLOXINIA (C): Beg in center, ch 5; do not join.

Rnd 1: Work 10 trc in fifth ch from hook; join with sl st to top of ch-4 at beg of rnd.

Rnd 2: Ch 4, trc in same st as sl st; * trc in next trc, 2 trc in next trc; rep from * 3 times more; end trc in each of last 2 trc; join with sl st to top of beg ch-4—16 trc, counting beg ch-4 as trc.

continued

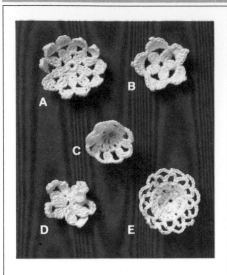

Note: For ease in working, turn work inside out.

Rnd 3: Ch 3, in same st as sl st work 2 dc; * ch 3, sk trc, 3 dc in next trc; rep from * around; end ch 3; join to top of ch-3 at beg of rnd—8 ch-3 lps.

Rnd 4: Sc in next dc; * in next ch-3 sp work **3 sc, ch 2, sl st in last sc made, and 2 sc—petal with picot made;** sc in center dc of next 3-dc grp; rep from * around. Join to first sc; fasten off.

CLUSTER FLOWER (D): Ch 5, join with sl st to form ring.

Rnd 1: * Ch 4, **holding last lp of each trc on hook, work 3 trc in ring, yo, draw through all 4 lps on hook—trc-cl made;** (ch 5, work trc-cl in fifth ch from hook) 2 times; sl st into ch-5 ring—one flower petal. Rep from * 4 times more; fasten off.

PETUNIA (E): Beg at center, ch 4; join with sl st to form ring.

Rnd 1: (Ch 4, trc in ring, ch 4, sl st in ring) 5 times.

Rnd 2: Sl st into next 4 ch; sc in first trc; (ch 4, sc in next trc) 4 times, ch 4; join to first sc.

Rnd 3: Sl st into ch-4 lp; ch 3, work 5 dc in same lp; (5 dc in next ch-5 lp) 4 times; join to top of ch-3 at beg of rnd—26 dc, counting beg ch-3 as dc.

Rnd 4: Ch 1, sc in same st as join; (ch 4, sk dc, sc in next dc) 12 times, ch 2, dc in sc at beg of rnd.

Rnd 5: Ch 1, sc in lp just made, (ch 5, sc in next lp) 12 times, ch 5, join to sc at beg of rnd; fasten off.

Primrose Filet Edging

Shown on page 7.

Edging is 1¾ inches wide.

MATERIALS
Coats & Clark Big Ball mercerized crochet cotton, Size 30 (300-yard ball): 1 ball of white or ecru
Size 13 steel crochet hook
Table runner 8¼x52 inches or desired size

Abbreviations: See page 78.
Gauge: 7 blocks = 1 inch.

INSTRUCTIONS
Note: Make the edging in one piece, adjusting its size to fit any table runner. Work the piece from side to side. Work filled blocks with 2 dc, plus dc on each side. When working from the chart, *right,* work odd-numbered rows from right to left; work even-numbered rows from left to right.

Beginning at Row 1 on chart, ch 41.

Row 1 (right side): Dc in eighth ch from hook, (ch 2, sk 2 ch, dc in next ch) 4 times; dc in next 3 ch, ch 2, sk 2 ch, dc in next 4 ch, (ch 2, sk 2 ch, dc in next ch) 4 times; ch 3, turn.

Row 2: (2 dc in ch-2 sp, dc in next dc) 2 times; (ch 2, dc in next dc) 2 times; ch 2, sk 2 dc, dc in next dc, ch 2, dc in next dc, ch 2, sk 2 dc, dc in next dc, 2 dc in ch-2 sp, dc in next dc, (ch 2, dc in next dc) 3 times; ch 2, sk 2 ch of turning-ch, dc in next ch; ch 5, turn.

Row 3: Sk first dc, dc in next dc, (ch 2, dc in next dc) 2 times; 2 dc in ch-2 sp, dc in next dc, ch 2, sk 2 dc, dc in next dc, (ch 2, dc in next dc) 5 times; ch 2, sk 2 dc, dc in next dc, ch 2, sk 2 dc, dc in top of turning ch-3; ch 3, turn.

Row 4: (2 dc in ch-2 sp, dc in next dc) 2 times, (ch 2, dc in next dc) 6 times, ch 2, sk 2 dc, dc in next dc, 2 dc in ch-2 sp, dc in next dc, ch 2, dc in next dc, ch 2, sk 2 ch of turning lp, dc in next ch; ch 5, turn.

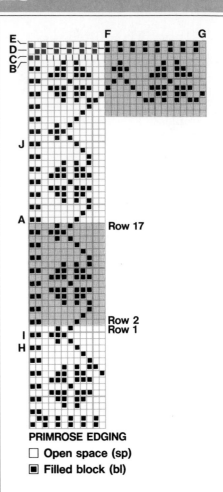

PRIMROSE EDGING
☐ **Open space (sp)**
■ **Filled block (bl)**

Rows 5–17: Work from chart. Rep rows 2–17 nineteen times more or for desired fabric length minus 2½ inches. Then work from Row A to Row B (do not work the shaded area between rows F and G) to complete side; ch 3, turn.

CORNER SHAPING: Rows C, D, and E are worked at the same time as follows:

Row 1: (2 dc in ch-2 sp, dc in next dc) 2 times; ch 3, turn.

Row 2: Sk first 3 dc, dc in next dc, ch 2, sk 2 dc, dc in top of ch-3; ch 3, turn.

Row 3: 2 dc in ch-2 sp, dc in next dc, 2 dc in next ch-3 turning-sp; dc in side of dc of Row B (two rows below), under two top lps. Ch 3, turn.

Row 4: Rep Row 2.

Row 5: 2 dc in sp, dc in next dc, 3 dc in next ch-2 sp of Row B, dc in next dc of Row B; ch 2, dc in next dc in Row B; ch 2, turn.

Row 6: Sk 5 dc and rep Row 2.

Row 7: (2 dc in ch-2 sp, dc in next dc) 2 times. *Note:* Last dc is worked in top lps at side of dc directly below. Dc in first dc of 4-dc grp in Row B, ch 2, sk 2 dc, dc in next dc of Row B; ch 2, turn.

Row 8: Sk 5 dc and rep Row 2.

Row 9: (2 dc in ch-2 sp, dc in next dc) 2 times; dc in first dc of next 4-dc grp in Row B, ch 2, sk 2 dc, dc in next dc of Row B; ch 2, turn.

Row 10: Sk 5 dc and rep Row 2.

Row 11: (2 dc in ch-2 sp, dc in next dc) 2 times; dc in next dc in Row B, ch 2, dc in next dc in Row B; ch 2, turn.

Row 12: Sk 5 dc and rep Row 2.

Row 13: Rep Row 11, except work last dc in Row B in third ch of turning ch-5; ch 2, turn.

Row 14: Sk 5 dc and rep Row 2; ch 3, turn.

NEXT SIDE: Begin next side at Row F on chart, then work through Row G. Rep rows F and G 11 times or for desired length minus 1 inch. Then rep rows J–B and work Corner Shaping to complete next side.

Continue to work as established for rem two sides. Work from rows H–I to complete first side; fasten off. Whipstitch edges together and sew edging to cloth.

Picket-Fence Edging

Shown on page 6.

Edging measures 4 inches at its widest point.

MATERIALS
Coats & Clark Big Ball
    mercerized crochet cotton,
    Size 30 (500-yard ball): 1 ball
    makes 3 yards
Size 13 steel crochet hook
Linen fabric 15x24 inches

Abbreviations: See page 78.
INSTRUCTIONS

Note: Work the edging from side to side until the desired length is reached. Add the mitered corners to both edges of both long strips and to both edges of both short strips. Hand-sew the mitered edges together to complete the piece.

LONG STRIP: Beginning at one of the narrow edges, ch 76.

Row 1 (wrong side): Dc in fourth and fifth ch from hook; ch 1, sk ch, dc in next 4 ch; (ch 2, sk 2 ch, dc in next ch) 15 times; dc in next 6 ch, ch 5, sk 5 ch, dc in next 10 ch; ch 3, turn.

Row 2: Sk first 3 dc, dc in next 7 dc, 3 dc in ch-5 sp, ch 5, sk 3 dc, dc in next 4 dc, 2 dc in ch-2 sp, dc in next dc, (ch 2, dc in next dc) 14 times, dc in next 3 dc, ch 1, dc in last 2 dc and top of turning-ch; ch 3, turn.

Row 3: Sk first dc, dc in next 2 dc, ch 1, dc in next 4 dc, (ch 2, dc in next dc) 13 times; 2 dc in ch-2 sp, dc in next 4 dc, ch 5, 3 dc in ch-5 sp, dc next 7 dc; ch 3, turn.

Row 4: Sk first 3 dc, dc in next 7 dc, 3 dc in ch-5 sp, ch 5, sk 3 dc, dc in next 4 dc, (2 dc in ch-2 sp, dc in dc) 11 times; (ch 2, dc in next dc) 2 times, dc in next 3 dc, ch 1, dc in next 2 dc and top of turning-ch; ch 3, turn.

Row 5: Sk first dc, dc in next 2 dc, ch 1, dc in next 4 dc, (ch 2, dc in next dc) 2 times; dc in 3 dc, (ch 5, sk 5 dc, dc in next dc) 5 times; ch 5, 3 dc in ch-5 sp, dc in next 7 dc; ch 8, turn.

Row 6: Dc in sixth, seventh, and eighth ch from hook, dc in next 7 dc, ch 5, 3 dc in ch-5 sp, (dc in next dc, 5 dc in ch-5 sp) 5 times; dc in next 4 dc, (ch 2, dc in next dc) 2 times; dc in next 3 dc, ch 1, dc in next 2 dc and top of turning-ch; ch 3, turn.

Row 7: Sk first dc, dc in next 2 dc, ch 1, dc in next 4 dc, (ch 2, dc in next dc) 2 times; (ch 2, sk 2 dc, dc in next dc) 11 times; dc in next 3 dc, 3 dc in ch-5 lp, ch 5, sk 3 dc, dc in next 7 dc, 3 dc in turning lp; ch 8, turn.

Row 8: Dc in sixth, seventh, and eighth ch from hook, dc in next 7 dc, ch 5, 3 dc in ch-5 lp, dc in next 4 dc, ch 2, sk 2 dc, dc in

next dc, (ch 2, dc in next dc) 13 times; dc in next 3 dc, ch 1, dc in next 2 dc and top of turning-ch; ch 3, turn.

Row 9: Sk first dc, dc in next 2 dc, ch 1, dc in next 4 dc, (ch 2, dc in next dc) 14 times; ch 2, sk 2 dc, dc in next 4 dc, 3 dc in ch-5 lp, ch 5, sk 3 dc, dc in 7 dc, 3 dc in turning lp; ch 3, turn.

Rep rows 2–9 seventeen times more or to desired length. When piece is appropriate length, follow instructions for Mitered Corner.

MITERED CORNER: *Row 1:* Work same as Row 2 of Long Strip to last 4-dc grp, then dc in next dc, hdc in next dc, draw up lp in each of next 2 dc, yo, draw through 3 lps on hook; sl st in ch-1 sp; turn.

Row 2: Sl st to first dc, ch 3 (to count as first dc), dc in next dc; work Row 3 of Long Strip beg at ( )s, except rep bet ( )s 12 times instead of 13.

Row 3: Work same as Row 4 of Long Strip to last filled bl; sk next ch-2 sp, dc in next dc; ch 3, turn.

Row 4: Sk 4 dc, dc in next dc; work same as Row 5 of Long Strip beg at second set of ( )s.

Row 5: Work same as Row 6 of Long Strip until four 5-dc grp are completed; 3 dc in last ch-5 sp, dc in next dc; ch 3, turn.

Row 6: Sk 4 dc, dc in next dc; work Row 7 of Long Strip beg at second set of ( )s, except rep bet ( )s 8 times instead of 11.

Row 7: Rep Row 8 of Long Strip, except rep bet ( )s 7 times instead of 13; dc in next dc; ch 3, turn.

Row 8: Sk next ch-2 sp, dc in next dc; complete row same as Row 9 of Long Strip beg at ( )s and rep bet ( )s 7 times.

Row 9: Work same as Row 2 of Long Strip, except rep bet ( )s 6 times instead of 14; sk ch-2 sp, dc in next dc; ch 3, turn.

Row 10: Sk ch-2 sp, dc in next dc; complete row same as Row 3 of Long Strip, except rep bet ( )s 4 times instead of 13.

continued

SPECIAL TREASURES

Row 11: Work same as Row 4 of Long Strip until 3 filled bl are completed; sk next ch-2 sp, dc in next dc; ch 3, turn.

Row 12: Sk 4 dc, dc in next dc; work same as Row 5 of Long Strip.

Row 13: Work same as Row 6 of Long Strip to ch-5 lp; ch 5, 3 dc in ch-5 lp, dc in dc, sk 2 ch, dc in next ch; ch 3, turn.

Row 14: Sk 4 dc, dc in last dc of grp, 3 dc in ch-5 lp; complete row same as Row 7 of Long Strip.

Row 15: Work same as Row 8 of Long Strip to ch-5 lp; ch 5, 3 dc in next ch-5 lp, dc in next dc, sk 2 dc, dc in next dc; ch 3, turn.

Row 16: Sk 4 dc, dc in last dc of grp, 3 dc in ch-5 lp, ch 5; complete row same as Row 9 of Long Strip.

Row 17: Work same as Row 2 of Long Strip to ch-5 lp; 3 dc in ch-5 lp, dc in last dc of next dc-grp; ch 3, turn.

Row 18: Sk 3 dc, dc in 4 dc; fasten off.

OPPOSITE CORNER: *Row 1:* Turn piece to edge of starting ch, sk 2 dc and the ch-1 along the straight edge; join thread with sc in next dc; work same as Row 1 of Mitered Corner.

Rows 2–18: Work same as Mitered Corner; fasten off.

Work another Long Strip, adding Mitered Corners to this piece.

SHORT STRIP (make 2): Work same as Long Strip until 11 pat rep are completed; work corners same as Long Strip.

FINISHING: Place the Long and Short Strips parallel to each other and hand-sew the pieces together at corners.

BORDER: Join thread at tip of any point with sc and work ch-3 lps (sc, ch 3, sc) evenly spaced around; join to first sc. Sl st in ch-3 lp, ch 6, sl st in third ch from hook, dc in same lp; **ch 3, sl st in third ch from hook—picot made;** dc in same lp; * ch 2, dc in next lp, in same lp work (picot, dc) 2 times; rep from * around; end ch 2, join to third ch of beg ch-6. Fasten off. Hand-sew the edging to the linen piece.

Five-Petal Doily

Shown on page 8.

Doily is 9 inches in diameter.

MATERIALS
Coats & Clark Big Ball mercerized crochet cotton, Size 10 (325-yard ball): 1 ball of white
Size 9 steel crochet hook

Abbreviations: See page 78.

INSTRUCTIONS
Beg in center, ch 6, join with sl st to form ring.

Rnd 1: Ch 3, work 19 dc in ring; join with sl st in top of ch-3 at beg of rnd.

Rnd 2: Ch 1, sc in same st as join; (ch 5, sk dc, sc in next dc) 9 times, ch 2, dc in sc at beg of rnd—10 ch-lps.

Rnd 3: Ch 1, sc in lp just made; (ch 6, sc in next ch-5 lp) 9 times, ch 6, join with sl st to beg sc.

Rnd 4: Sl st into next ch-6 lp, ch 4, in same lp work 5 trc; in each ch-6 lp around work 6 trc; join with sl st in top of beg ch-4.

Rnd 5: Ch 3, dc in next 11 trc; * ch 4, dc in next 12 trc; rep from * 3 times more; end ch 4, join to top of ch-3 at beg of rnd.

Rnd 6: Sl st into next dc, ch 3, dc in same dc, dc in next 10 dc; * ch 4, sc in ch-4 lp, ch 4, sk first dc on 12-dc grp, 2 dc in next dc, dc in next 10 dc; rep from * 3 times more; end ch 4, sc in last ch-4 lp, ch 4, join to top of ch-3 at beg of rnd—12 dc in each dc-grp.

Rnd 7: Sl st into next dc, ch 3, dc in next 10 dc; * (ch 5, sc in next ch-4 lp) 2 times, ch 5, sk first dc on dc-grp, dc in next 11 dc; rep from * 3 times more; end (ch 5, sc in next ch-4 lp) 2 times, ch 5, join to top of ch-3—11 dc in each dc-grp.

Rnd 8: Sl st into next dc, ch 3, dc in next 9 dc; * (ch 5, sc in next ch-5 lp) 3 times, ch 5, sk first dc on dc-grp, dc in next 10 dc; rep from * 3 times more; end (ch 5, sc in next ch-5 lp) 3 times, ch 5, join in top of beg ch-3—10 dc in each dc-grp.

Rnd 9: Sl st into next dc, ch 3, dc in next 7 dc; * (ch 5, sc in next ch-5 lp) 4 times, ch 5, sk first dc on next dc-grp, dc in next 8 dc; rep from * 3 times more; end (ch 5, sc in next ch-5 lp) 4 times, ch 5, join in top of beg ch-3.

Rnd 10: Sl st into next dc, ch 3, holding back last lp of each dc, dc in next 5 dc, yo, draw through all lps on hook, ch 1 tightly; * (ch 5, sc in next ch-5 lp) 5 times, ch 5, sk first dc on next dc-grp, **holding back last lp of each dc, dc in next 6 dc, yo, draw through all lps on hook, ch 1 tightly—cl made;** rep from * 3 times more; end (ch 5, sc in next ch-5 lp) 5 times, ch 2, dc in top of beg cl—6 ch-5 lps bet cl.

Rnd 11: Ch 1, sc in lp just made, * ch 6, sc in next ch-5 lp; rep from * around; end ch 3, dc in sc at beg of rnd.

Rnd 12: Ch 1, sc in lp just made, * ch 7, sc in next ch-6 lp; rep from * around; end ch 4, dc in sc at beg of rnd.

Rnd 13: Ch 4, 3 trc in lp just made; * ch 3, 4 trc in next ch-7 lp; rep from * around; end ch 3, join in top of beg ch-4.

Rnd 14: Sl st into next 3 trc and into ch-3 sp; ch 4, 3 trc in same sp; * ch 3, 4 trc in next ch-3 sp; rep from * around; end ch 3, join in top of beg ch-4.

Rnd 15: Sl st into next 3 trc and into first 2 ch of ch-3 lp, ch 1, sc in same lp; * ch 5, sc between second and third trc of next 4-trc grp, ch 5, sc in next ch-3 lp; rep from * around; end ch 2, dc in beg sc.

Rnds 16–18: Ch 1, sc in lp just made; * ch 6, sc in next ch-lp; rep from * around; end ch 3, dc in sc at beg of rnd.

Rnd 19: Rep Rnd 16, except end row with ch 6, join with sl st in sc at beg of rnd.

Rnd 20: Ch 4, 4 trc in next ch-6 sp; * trc in next sc, 4 trc in next ch-6 lp; rep from * around; join to top of beg ch-4.

Rnd 21: Ch 1, sc in same st as join; * sk next 4 trc, dtr in next trc, **ch 3, sl st into dtr just made—picot made;** in same st work (dtr, picot) 4 times and dtr; sk 4 trc, sc in next trc; rep from * around; join to beg sc. Fasten off.

Rose Filet Doily

Shown on page 9.

Doily measures about 23 inches at its widest point.

MATERIALS
J. & P. Coats Knit-Cro-Sheen crochet thread (250-yard ball): 2 balls of white or ecru
Size 7 steel crochet hook

Abbreviations: See page 78.
Gauge: 11 dc = 1 inch.

INSTRUCTIONS
Note: This doily is recommended for experienced crocheters only.

When working from the chart, *below,* you'll make two different size blocks: A filled ch-2 block contains 2 dc plus a dc at each side; a filled ch-5 block contains 5 dc plus a dc at each side. A half-filled ch-5 block contains 3 dc and 1 side dc.

DOILY: Beginning at bottom of doily, ch 21.
Row 1: Dc in fourth ch from hook and in each ch across—19 dc, counting turning-ch as stitch, or 6 filled bl; ch 8, turn.
Row 2: Dc in fourth ch from hook and in next 4 ch; dc in next *continued*

Row 90

Row 1

ROSE FILET DOILY

☐ Open space (sp)
■ Filled block (bl)
▭ Ch-5 open space

dc, (ch 2, sk 2 dc, dc in next dc) 5 times, ch 2, dc in top of turning-ch. **Yo, draw up a lp in the base of the last dc made, yo, draw through 1 lp on hook (ch-1 made at bottom of st); complete st as a dc—dc-inc at end of row made;** working into the ch-1 st at base of last st, work 5 more dc-inc sts; ch 5, turn.

Row 3: Dc in fourth and fifth ch from hook, dc in next dc, (ch 2, sk 2 dc, dc in next dc) 2 times; (2 dc in next ch-2 sp, dc in next dc) 6 times; (ch 2, sk 2 dc, dc in next dc) 2 times; work 3 dc-inc at end of row; ch 3, turn.

Row 4: Sk first dc, dc in next 3 dc, ch 2, dc in next dc, 2 dc in ch-2 lp, dc in next dc, ch 2, sk 2 dc, dc in next dc, **(ch 5, sk 5 dc, dc in next dc—ch-5 sp made) 2 times;** ch 2, sk 2 dc, dc in next dc, 2 dc in ch-2 lp, dc in next dc, ch 2, dc in next 3 dc and top of turning-ch; ch 17, turn.

Row 5: Dc in fourth ch from hook and in next 8 ch—3 bl; ch 2, sk 2 ch, dc in next ch; dc in next 2 ch, dc in next dc; ch 2, sk 2 dc, dc in next ch; 2 dc in ch-2 sp, dc in dc, ch 2, sk 2 dc, dc in next dc, ch 5, 3 dc in ch-5 lp, dc in next dc, ch 2, dc in ch-5 lp, ch 5, sk dc, dc in next dc, ch 2, sk 2 dc, dc in next dc, 2 dc in ch-2 lp, dc in dc, ch 2, sk 2 dc, dc in top of turning-ch; work 3 dc-inc; **ch 2, yo, draw up lp at base of last st, (yo, draw through 1 lp on hook) 2 times; complete st as a dc—open-bl inc made at end of row;** work 9 dc-inc; ch 5, turn.

Continue to work from chart, page 17. Read odd-numbered rows from right to left and even-numbered rows from left to right.

For rows 7 and 8, do not work the shaded portions of the chart. Work these portions of the doily separately when all other chart work is completed.

When increases are made at the beg of a row, work the number of ch to accommodate each stitch or block, then add two more ch for the turning. For example, for a 4-block increase, ch 14 (3 sts per block multiplied by 4 blocks equals 12, plus 2 turning ch). To increase 10 blocks, as in Row 9, ch 32 at the end of Row 8.

To decrease at the beginning of a row, slip-stitch across the required number of stitches. Then ch 3 to begin the row, counting the ch 3 as the first dc.

To decrease at the end of a row, leave stitches unworked. Ch 3 and turn.

Work from chart through Row 90; fasten off. Referring to chart, join thread at corners and work each shaded area separately.

BORDER: Sc evenly around entire piece. At outside corners, work 3 sc. At inside corners, draw up a lp in st before corner, draw up a lp in st after corner, yo, draw through 3 lps on hook. Continue around in this manner; join to first sc. Fasten off.

Sawtooth-Lace Edging

Shown on page 11.

Pillow is about 22 inches in diameter, including ruffle. Edging is about 5 inches at its widest point.

MATERIALS
Clark mercerized crochet cotton, Size 20 (300-yard ball): 1 ball of white or ecru
Size 10 steel crochet hook
½ yard of printed chintz for pillow top
1½ yards of green chintz for pillow back and ruffle
1¼ yards of narrow pink satin twisted cord
2 yards each of pink and rose ⅜-inch-wide satin ribbons
Polyester fiberfill

Abbreviations: See page 78.
Gauge: 10 dc = 1 inch.

INSTRUCTIONS
Beg at one of the narrow edges, ch 38.

Row 1: Dc in fourth ch from hook, ch 5, sk 5 ch, in next ch work **2 dc, ch 2, and 2 dc—shell made;** ch 1, sk 2 ch, shell in next ch; ch 1, sk ch, 2 dc in next ch, dc in next 8 ch, (ch 2, sk 2 ch, in next ch work **dc, ch 1, and dc—V st made**) 5 times; ch 3, turn.

Row 2: (Work shell in ch-1 sp of next V st, ch 1) 4 times; shell in next ch-1 sp of V st, ch 2, dc in first dc of 10-dc grp and in next 9 dc, 2 dc in ch-1 sp; (ch 1, shell in ch-2 sp of next shell) 2 times; ch 5, dc in last dc and top of turning-ch; ch 3, turn.

Row 3: Sk first dc, dc in next dc, ch 5, (shell in ch-2 sp of next shell, ch 1) 2 times; 2 dc in ch-1 sp, dc in next 12 dc, ch 2, (shell in ch-2 sp of next shell, ch 1) 4 times; shell in ch-2 sp of last shell; ch 3, turn.

Row 4: (Work shell in ch-2 sp of next shell, ch 1) 4 times, shell in ch-2 sp of shell, ch 2, dc in first dc of 14-dc grp and in next 13 dc; 2 dc in ch-1 sp, (ch 1, shell in ch-2 sp of next shell) 2 times; ch 5, dc in last dc and top of turning-ch; ch 3, turn.

Row 5: Rep Row 3, except dc in 16 dc instead of 12; ch 3, turn.

Row 6: Rep Row 4, except dc in 18 dc instead of 14; ch 3, turn.

Row 7: Rep Row 3, except dc in 20 dc instead of 12; ch 3, turn.

Row 8: Rep Row 4, except dc in 22 dc instead of 14; ch 3, turn.

Row 9: Sk first dc, dc in next dc, ch 5, (shell in ch-2 sp of next shell, ch 1) 2 times; 2 dc in ch-1 sp, dc in next 8 dc, (ch 2, sk 2 dc, V st in next dc) 4 times, ch 2, sk 3 dc, V st in next dc; ch 3, turn.

Rep rows 2–9 for pat until 22 points are completed or for desired length, ending with Row 8; fasten off.

TOP EDGING: *Row 1:* With wrong side facing and piece turned so you can work across one of the long straight edges, work 2 sc in each dc post (turning ch-3) across; ch 1, turn.
Row 2: Sc in each sc across; fasten off.

FINISHING: Wash edging and starch lightly. Pin to measurements and allow to dry. From print chintz, cut one 15-inch-diameter circle for pillow top. Cut another circle the same size from green chintz for pillow back. Set pieces aside.

For the ruffle, cut enough 12-inch-wide strips to make four yards. Sew pieces together to form a tube. Fold strip in half lengthwise, with wrong sides facing; steam-press. Sew a double line of gathering stitches ¼ inch from raw edges. Draw threads to gather ruffle to fit pillow top.

Baste ruffle to pillow top. With right sides facing, sew pillow top to pillow back, leaving an opening for turning. Clip seams and turn right side out. Stuff pillow with fiberfill and sew opening closed.

Whipstitch the short ends of the crocheted piece together. Hand-sew the edging around the pillow. Hand-sew the cording atop the crochet edges.

Cut each piece of ribbon into two 1-yard lengths. Holding one piece of pink ribbon and one piece of rose ribbon together as one, lace the ribbons through the ch-5 lps; lace until half of edging is threaded. Working in the same manner, lace the other two pieces on the rem half of the edging. Tie ribbon ends into bows. Trim ribbon ends to desired length.

Lily-of-the-Valley Doily Pillow

Shown on page 10.

Doily measures about 14 inches in diameter.

MATERIALS
J. & P. Coats Knit-Cro-Sheen (325-yard ball): 1 ball of white or ecru
Size 7 steel crochet hook
½ yard rose chintz for pillow top and back
¾ yard of yellow-print chintz for ruffle
½ yard of solid-yellow chintz for piping
1¼ yards of narrow piping cord
Polyester fiberfill

Abbreviations: See page 78.
Gauge: Rnds 1 and 2 = 1½ inches in diameter.

INSTRUCTIONS
DOILY: Beg at center, ch 6; join with sl st to form ring.

Rnd 1: Ch 5, (dc in ring, ch 2) 7 times; join with sl st to third ch of beg ch-5—8 ch-2 lps.

Rnd 2: Sl st in ch-2 lp, ch 3, **retaining last lp of each st on hook, work 4 trc in same sp, yo, and draw through all lps on hook—beg cl made;** * ch 4, **retaining last lp of each st on hook, work 5 trc in next ch-2 sp, yo, and draw through all lps on hook—cl made;** rep from * 6 times more; end ch 4, join with sl st to top of first cl—8 cl.

Rnd 3: Sl st in next ch-4 lp, ch 4; in same lp work 2 trc, ch 2, and 3 trc; * ch 3, in next ch-4 lp work 3 trc, ch 2, and 3 trc; rep from * 6 times more; end ch 3, sl st in top of beg ch-4.

Rnd 4: Ch 4, trc in same st as join, trc in next 2 trc, ch 2, trc in next 2 trc, 2 trc in next trc; * ch 3, 2 trc in next trc, trc in next 2 trc, ch 2, trc in next 2 trc, 2 trc in next trc; rep from * 6 times more; end ch 3, join to top of beg ch-4.

Rnd 5: Ch 4, trc in same st as join, trc in next 3 trc; ch 2, trc in next 3 trc, 2 trc in next trc; * ch 3, 2 trc in next trc, trc in next 3 trc, ch 2, trc in next 3 trc, 2 trc in next trc; rep from * 6 times more; end ch 3, join to top of beg ch-4.

Rnd 6: Ch 4, trc in next 4 trc, ch 2, trc in next 5 trc; * ch 2, trc in next ch-3 lp, ch 2, trc in next 5 trc, ch 2, trc in next 5 trc; rep from * 6 times more; end ch 2, trc in next ch-3 lp, ch 2, join to top of beg ch-4.

Rnd 7: Ch 3, trc in next 4 trc, ch 2, trc in next 3 trc; **retaining last lp of each st on hook, trc in next 2 trc, yo, and draw through all lps on hook—trc-dec made;** * ch 3, sk next ch-2 lp, trc in next ch-2 lp, ch 2, 2 trc in first trc of 5-trc grp; ch 2, work trc-dec over first and second trc of same 5-trc grp, trc in next 3 trc, ch 2, trc in next 3 trc, work trc-dec over next 2 trc; rep from * 6 times more; end ch 2, sk next ch-2 lp, trc in next ch-2 lp, ch 2, 2 trc in same ch used as join for previous rnd; ch 2, join to top of first trc (sk beg ch-3).

Rnd 8: Ch 3, trc in next 5 trc, trc-dec over next 2 trc; * ch 3, sk next ch-2 lp, trc in next ch-2 lp, ch 2, trc in 2 trc, ch 2, trc in ch-2 lp, ch 2 **, trc-dec over next 2 trc, trc in next 4 trc, trc-dec over next 2 trc; rep from * around, ending at ** on last rep; join last ch-2 to top of first trc.

Rnd 9: Ch 3, trc in next 3 trc, trc-dec over next 2 trc; * (ch 3, trc in next ch-lp) 2 times; ch 2, in next trc work 2 trc, ch 2; in next trc work 2 trc, ch 1, and 2 trc; ch 3, sk ch-lp, trc in next lp, ch 3 **, trc-dec over next 2 trc, trc in next 2 trc, trc-dec over next 2 trc; rep from * around, ending at ** on last rep; join last ch-3 to top of first trc.

Rnd 10: Ch 3, **retaining last lp of each trc on hook, trc in next 3 trc, yo, and draw through all lps on hook—beg trc-cl made;** * (ch 3, trc in next ch-lp) 2 times, ch 3, sk next trc, trc in next 2 trc, ch 3, 2 trc in next trc, trc in next trc, ch 2, trc in next trc, 2 trc in next trc, ch 3, sk next ch-lp, trc in next lp, ch 3 **, **retaining last lp of each trc on hook, trc in next 4 trc, yo, and draw through all lps on hook—4-trc cl made;** rep from * around, ending at ** on last rep; join last ch-3 to top of first cl.

Rnd 11: Ch 7, trc in next ch-sp, * ch 3, **retaining last lp of each st on hook, work 6 trc in next ch-sp, yo, and draw through all lps on hook—6-trc cl made;** ch 1, sk next ch-lp, trc in next 2 trc, ch 2, trc in next ch-lp, ch 2, 2 trc in next trc, trc in next 2 trc, ch 2, trc in next 2 trc, 2 trc in next trc, ch 3, sk next lp, trc in next lp, ch 3 **, trc in trc-cl, ch 3, trc in next ch-lp; rep from * around, ending at ** on last rep; join with sl st to fourth ch of beg ch-7.

Rnd 12: Sl st into next 2 ch of ch-3 lp, ch 7, trc in next lp, * ch 1, sk cl, trc in next 2 trc, (ch 3, trc in next lp) 2 times, ch 2; in next trc work 2 trc, ch 3, and 2 trc; trc in next 3 trc, ch 2, trc in next 3 trc, 2 trc in next trc, ch 3, sk next lp, trc in next lp **, (ch 3, trc in next lp) 2 times; rep from * around, ending at ** on last rep; ch 3, join to fourth ch of beg ch-7.

continued

Rnd 13: Sl st in first ch of ch-3 lp, ch 3, work 5-trc cl in same lp, * ch 1, trc in next 2 trc, (ch 3, trc in next ch-lp) 2 times; ch 1, sk next lp, trc in next 2 trc, ch 2, trc in next ch-lp, ch 2, trc in next 5 trc, ch 2, trc in next 5 trc, (ch 3, trc in next lp) 2 times; ch 3 **, 6-trc cl in next ch-lp; rep from * around, ending at ** on last rep; join last ch-3 with sl st to top of first cl.

Rnd 14: Sl st to next trc, ch 4, trc in next trc; * ch 3, trc in next lp, ch 3, 6-trc cl in next lp; ch 1, sk next trc, trc in next 2 trc, (ch 3, trc in next lp) 2 times, ch 3, trc-dec over next 2 trc, trc in next 6 trc, trc-dec over next 2 trc; (ch 3, trc in next lp) 3 times, ch 1 **, sk cl, trc in next 2 trc; rep from * around, ending at ** on last rep; join last ch-1 with sl st to top of beg ch-4.

Rnd 15: Ch 4, trc in next trc; * (ch 3, trc in next lp) 2 times, ch 3, sk cl, trc in next 2 trc, (ch 3, trc in next lp) 3 times, ch 3, trc-dec over next 2 trc, trc in next 4 trc, trc-dec over next 2 trc, (ch 3, trc in next lp) 2 times, ch 3, 6-trc cl in next lp, ch 1 **, sk trc, trc in next 2 trc; rep from * around, ending at ** on last rep; join last ch-1 with sl st to top of beg ch-4.

Rnd 16: Ch 4, trc in next trc; * ch 3, trc in next lp, ch 3, 6-trc cl in next lp, ch 1, sk trc, trc in next 2 trc, (ch 3, trc in next lp) 4 times, ch 3, trc-dec over next 2 trc, trc in next 2 trc, trc-dec over next 2 trc; (ch 3, trc in next lp) 3 times, ch 3 **, sk cl, trc in next 2 trc; rep from * around, ending at ** on last rep; join last ch-3 to top of beg ch-4.

Rnd 17: Ch 4, trc in next trc; * (ch 3, trc in next lp) 2 times, ch 3, sk cl, trc in next 2 trc, (ch 3, trc in next lp) 5 times, ch 3, 4-trc cl in next 4 trc; (ch 3, trc in next lp) 2 times, ch 3, 6-trc cl in next lp, ch 1 **, sk trc, trc in next 2 trc; rep from * around, ending at ** on last rep; join to top of beg ch-4.

Rnd 18: Sl st into next trc, ch 7, trc in next lp, (ch 3, trc in next lp) 2 times; * ch 3, sk trc, trc in next trc, (ch 3, trc in next lp) 6 times, ch 3, trc in next cl, (ch 3, trc in next lp) 3 times, ch 3 **, sk trc, trc in next trc; (ch 3, trc in next lp) 3 times; rep from * around, ending at ** on last rep; join last ch-3 to fourth ch of beg ch-7.

Rnd 19: Sl st into next lp, ch 3, 4 dc in same lp, * 4 sc in next lp, 5 dc in next lp; rep from * around; join to top of ch-3 at beg of rnd; fasten off.

FINISHING: Wash doily and starch lightly. Pin to measurements, taking care to have eight evenly spaced sides; let dry.

Place doily on rose chintz. Lightly draw a line around doily ¾ inch beyond all sides. Cut two pieces from fabric for pillow top and back.

For the piping, cut a 1¼-inch-wide strip of 44-inch-long solid-yellow chintz. Cover cotton cording with strip using zipper foot. Sew piping to pillow top with right sides facing. Trim excess fabric.

For the ruffle, cut a 6-inch-wide strip from the yellow-print chintz; cut enough strips to make 4¼ yards. Using ¼-inch seams, sew pieces into one long strip. Fold strip in half with wrong sides together and steam-press. Gather ruffle on machine.

Baste ruffle in place around pillow top. With right sides facing, sew pillow top to pillow back, leaving an opening for turning. Stuff pillow and sew opening closed. Stretching slightly, sew doily in place on pillow top.

Filet-Rose Pillow

Shown on page 10.

Pillow measures about 11x13 inches without the ruffle.

MATERIALS

Clark's mercerized crochet cotton, Size 30 (300-yard ball): 1 ball of white or ecru
Size 12 steel crochet hook
½ yard green chintz for pillow top and back
¾ yard yellow-print chintz for ruffle
½ yard of solid-yellow chintz for piping
1½ yards of narrow cotton cording for piping
Polyester fiberfill

Abbreviations: See page 78.
Gauge: 12 dc = 1 inch.

INSTRUCTIONS

Note: Crochet is worked on 67 meshes; filled blocks are worked with 2 dc, plus the side dc.

Beginning along bottom, ch 203.

Row 1: Dc in fourth ch from hook and in next 46 ch—16 bl; (ch 2, sk 2 ch, dc in next ch) 13 times—13 sp; dc in next 6 ch, ch 2, sk 2 ch, dc in next 10 ch; ch 2, sk 2 ch, dc in next 7 ch, (ch 2, sk 2 ch, dc in next ch) 13 times; dc in next 48 ch; ch 3, turn.

Row 2: Sk first dc, dc in next 3 dc, (ch 2, sk 2 dc, dc in next dc) 4 times; dc in next 15 dc, ch 2, sk 2 dc, dc in next 4 dc; (ch 2, sk 2 dc, dc in next dc) 4 times; (ch 2, dc in next dc) 13 times; (ch 2, sk 2 dc, dc in next dc) 2 times; 2 dc in ch-2 sp, dc in next dc, ch 2, sk 2 dc, dc in next 4 dc, ch 2, sk 2 dc, dc in next dc, 2 dc in ch-2 sp, dc in next dc, (ch 2, sk 2 dc, dc in next dc) 2 times; (ch 2, dc in next dc) 13 times; (ch 2, sk 2 dc, dc in next dc) 4 times; dc in next 3 dc, ch 2, sk 2 dc, dc in next 16 dc, (ch 2, sk 2 dc, dc in next dc) 4 times, dc in next 2 dc, dc in top of turning ch; ch 3, turn.

Row 3: Sk first dc, dc in next 3 dc, ch 2, dc in next dc, 2 dc in ch-2 sp, dc in next dc, (ch 2, dc in next dc) 2 times; (ch 2, sk 2 dc, dc in next dc) 5 times; ch 2, dc in next dc, dc in next 3 dc; (ch 2, dc in next dc) 12 times; (2 dc in ch-2 sp, dc in next dc) 7 times; ch 2, sk 2 dc, dc in next dc, 2 dc in next ch-2 sp, dc in next 4 dc, 2 dc in ch-2 sp, dc in next dc, ch 2, sk 2 dc, dc in next dc; (2 dc in ch-2 sp, dc in next dc) 7 times; (ch 2, dc in next dc) 12 times; dc in next 3 dc, ch 2, dc in next dc; (ch 2, sk 2 dc, dc in next dc) 5 times; (ch 2, dc in next dc) 2 times; 2 dc in ch-2 sp, dc in next dc, ch 2, dc in next 3 dc, dc in top of turning ch-3; ch 3, turn.

Rows 4–16: Work from chart, *opposite.* Read odd-numbered rows from right to left and even-numbered rows from left to right. At end of Row 16, ch 5, turn.

Rows 17–67: Continue to work from chart. When rows begin with an open space, always ch 5 to turn at the end of the previous row, counting the chain as the first dc and ch-2 sp. When an open space is on top of an open space at the end of a row, work the last dc in the third ch of the turning ch-5.

When rows begin with a filled block, always ch 3 to turn at the end of the previous row. When a filled block is at the end of a row and over an open space, work 2 dc in the open space and dc in the third ch of the turning ch-5.

FINISHING: Wash the crocheted piece and starch lightly. Pin to measurements and allow to dry.

From green chintz, cut two rectangles, each 11½x14½ inches. From solid-yellow chintz, cut and piece 1¼-inch-wide bias strips to cover 48 inches of the corded piping. Cover cotton piping with strips using zipper foot. Baste piping to pillow top.

For the ruffle, cut 6-inch-wide strips from the yellow-print chintz. Piece strips together to form a 2¾-yard length; sew ends together. Fold ruffle in half lengthwise and run gathering threads ½ inch from raw edge. Gather ruffle to fit pillow top and baste in place.

With right sides together, sew back to top, leaving an opening for turning. Clip corners, turn, and stuff. Sew opening closed. Hand-sew the crocheted piece to the pillow top along the edges.

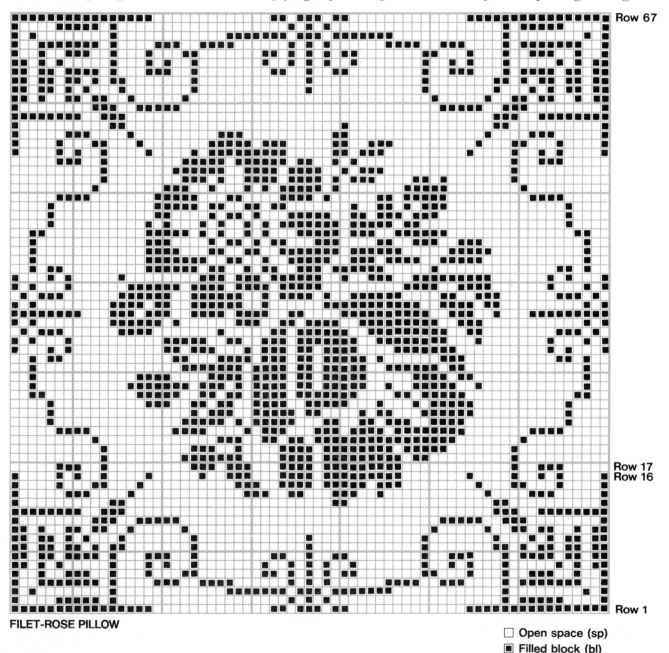

FILET-ROSE PILLOW

Row 67

Row 17
Row 16

Row 1

☐ **Open space (sp)**
■ **Filled block (bl)**

TABLE MATS AND LINENS

PLAIN AND FANCY

Whether your preference is for traditional sophistication, Victorian elegance, or unaffected country charm, you can create the atmosphere you want in your home with handcrafted linens. In this chapter you'll find an imaginative array of designs for your table, ranging from place mats stitched with yarn to lace cloths worthy of the most formal occasions.

Stitched in a traditional country pattern, the checked place mat, *left,* measures 13x19 inches. Work this design with two yarns at the same time, making the stitches with one yarn while carrying the other. Bobble stitches hide the thread you're not using and create the thick, cushiony surface.

The star-shaped mat, *below,* is an adaptation in yarn of the lace coaster on page 27. When crocheted with knitting worsted, the coaster pattern (with minor adjustments) works up to 16 inches in diameter.

Directions for projects begin on page 32.

TABLE MATS AND LINENS

Place mats of princely proportions are stunning on tables of any size. The oversize, 16x18-inch mat, *above*, for example, looks just as charming atop a small table as it would on a grand dining-room table.

Handsome filet crochet in a tailored, no-frills design gives this generously sized mat its great versatility. The center of the mat features bands of open and filled meshes that create diagonal furrows similar to the light-and-dark Straight Furrow design found in many traditional Log Cabin quilts.

Simple borders surround the center of the mat, and picots trim the outermost edges.

Work this design in sturdy bedspread cotton using a Size 7 hook.

The dessert mat *above* may be small—it measures only 9x13 inches—but it's every bit as charming as a larger mat would be. Use it at teatime, as shown here, or any time you need a touch of lace to set off a special treat or dress up a table.

If you're a beginning stitcher interested in learning how to work from a chart, try this filet crochet mat. The design is simple, with only 34 rows in the pattern, and the picot edging is uncomplicated. For ease in stitching, use the thread recommended in the instructions, or any Size 10 mercerized crochet cotton.

Plan ahead for a fancy party—that's what all the guides to great entertaining tell us. And there's no nicer way to prepare for an elegant dinner than by crafting some magnificent place mats for your table.

The lacy design, *opposite,* measures 14x20 inches. For each place mat, crochet and join six 6-inch-square blocks, then trim the assembled motifs with a 1-inch-deep edging.

Or, you could stitch a tablecloth—a project that *really* calls for planning ahead. Crochet sufficient blocks to cover the top of your table and allow for an eight- to ten-inch drop all around.

The coaster, *above,* is crocheted following the same instructions used for the large yarn mat on page 23. To make the smaller (six inches in diameter), more formal coaster, work the design in Size 10 crochet cotton.

The place mat, *above,* also is stitched in Size 10 thread. It measures 15¾ inches in diameter.

TABLE LINENS

A crocheted tablecloth *looks* like an enormous undertaking. But if you stitch in small segments, you'll find that you can create one rather quickly.

Just tuck your crochet cotton and hook into a bag to carry with you wherever you go. When you have a few spare moments—riding in a car or bus, waiting for an appointment, relaxing after lunch, watching television— crochet a few rounds. In practically no time, you'll have a stack of motifs ready to join into a beautiful cloth.

This star-bedecked, 62x80-inch cloth is assembled from more than 450 hexagon-shaped medallions. Worked in Size 20 thread, the medallions measure about 3½ inches between points.

Each motif contains only seven rounds. Using a Size 8 steel hook, work all seven for the first medallion. On succeeding blocks, work six rounds, then join the block to its neighbors on the seventh round.

A traditional pineapple design graces each of the 4½-inch-square blocks in the table runner, *above*. To crochet this 16x62-inch cloth, work 52 blocks and join them into 13 rows of four blocks each. (For place mats, work a dozen blocks; join into three rows of four blocks each.)

The daisylike pattern in the cloth, *opposite*, is reminiscent of sturdy Cluny laces rich with stylized flower designs. Here, in these hexagonal motifs, each flower has a dozen petals created and gracefully shaped with cluster stitches.

This 53x68-inch tablecloth contains 188 motifs. Measuring about five inches across, each motif is stitched in only 10 rounds.

Crochet the blocks individually. Whipstitch the finished blocks together, then finish the outer edges of this lovely cloth with a simple picot trim.

Yarn Mat And Thread Coaster

Yarn mat is shown on page 23; coaster is shown on page 27.

Mat is 16 inches in diameter; coaster is 6 inches in diameter.

MATERIALS
For the place mat
Unger Aries knitting worsted yarn (3½-ounce skein): 1 skein of off-white
Size H aluminum crochet hook

For the coaster
DMC Cebelia crochet cotton, Size 10 (50-gram ball): 1 ball of white
Size 7 steel crochet hook

Abbreviations: See page 78.

INSTRUCTIONS
Instructions are for both items. Work the instructions in the parentheses when crocheting the thread coaster. Where there are no parentheses, work as indicated for both projects.

Beginning at center, ch 5; join with sl st to form ring.

Rnd 1: Ch 1, sc in ring; * ch 7 (ch 6), sc in ring; rep from * 6 times more; end ch 7 (ch 6), join with sl st to first sc.

Rnd 2: Sl st in next 4 (3) ch, sc in same lp; * ch 3 (ch 4), sc in next lp; rep from * 6 times more; end ch 3 (ch 4), join with sl st in sc at beg of rnd.

Rnd 3: Ch 1, * in next ch-3 lp work 2 sc (3 sc), **ch 2, sl st in second ch from hook—picot made**, and 2 sc (3 sc), ch 1; rep from * around; join last ch-1 with sl st in first ch-1 sp.

Rnd 4: Ch 3, dc in same ch-1 sp; * ch 5 (ch 6), 2 dc in next ch-1 sp; rep from * 6 times more; end ch 5 (ch 6), join with sl st in top of ch-3 at beg of rnd.

Rnd 5: Sl st in next dc and into next ch-lp; ch 3, in same lp work 9 dc; * ch 1, in next ch-lp work 10 dc; rep from * 6 times more; end ch 1, join with sl st to top of ch-3 at beg of rnd.

Rnd 6: Sl st in next 5 dc, ch 6, dc in same st as last sl st; * ch 3 (ch 4), in next ch-1 sp work dc, ch 3, and dc; ch 3 (ch 4), sk 4 dc, in next dc work dc, ch 3, and dc; rep from * 6 times more; end ch 3 (ch 4), in next ch-1 sp work dc, ch 3, and dc; ch 3 (ch 4), join with sl st to third ch of ch-6 at beg of rnd.

Rnd 7: Sl st into next ch-3 lp; ch 3, in same lp work 2 dc, ch 2, and 3 dc; * ch 2 (ch 3), sk next ch-lp, in next ch-lp work 5 sc; ch 2 (ch 3), sk next ch-lp, in next ch-3 lp work 3 dc, ch 2, and 3 dc; rep from * 6 times more; end ch 2 (ch 3), sk next ch-lp, 5 sc in next ch-lp; ch 2 (ch 3), join with sl st to top of ch-3 at beg of rnd.

Rnd 8: Ch 3, dc in next 2 dc, in ch-2 sp work 2 dc, ch 2, and 2 dc; dc in next 3 dc; * ch 2 (ch 3), sk sc, sc in next 4 sc, ch 2 (ch 3), dc in next 3 dc, in next ch-2 sp work 2 dc, ch 2, and 2 dc; dc in next 3 dc; rep from * 6 times more; end ch 2 (ch 3), sk sc, sc in next 4 sc, ch 2 (ch 3), join to top of ch-3.

Rnd 9: Ch 3, dc in next 4 dc; in ch-2 sp work 2 dc, ch 2, and 2 dc; dc in next 5 dc; * ch 2 (ch 3), sk sc, sc in next 3 sc, ch 2 (ch 3), dc in next 5 dc; in ch-2 sp work 2 dc, ch 2, and 2 dc; dc in next 5 dc; rep from * 6 times more; end ch 2 (ch 3), sk sc, sc in next 3 sc, ch 2 (ch 3), join with sl st to top of ch-3.

Rnd 10: Ch 3, dc in next 6 dc; in ch-2 sp work 2 dc, ch 2, and 2 dc; dc in next 7 dc; * ch 2 (ch 3), sk sc, sc in 2 sc, ch 2 (ch 3), dc in next 7 dc, in ch-2 sp work 2 dc, ch 2, and 2 dc; dc in next 7 dc; rep from * 6 times more; end ch 2 (ch 3), sk sc, sc in 2 sc, ch 2 (ch 3), join with sl st to top of ch-3.

Note: The parentheses in the next two rounds include instructions for both the mat and coaster. Work the instructions as indicated for both projects.

Rnd 11: Ch 5, sk dc, dc in next dc; (ch 2, sk dc, dc in next dc) 3 times; * ch 2, dc in ch-2 lp, ch 2, dc in next dc, (ch 2, sk dc, dc in next dc) 4 times, sk 2 sc, dc in next dc, (ch 2, sk dc, dc in next dc) 4 times; rep from * 6 times more; end dc in ch-2 lp, ch 2, dc in next dc, (ch 2, sk dc, dc in next dc) 4 times, sk 2 sc, join with sl st to third ch of beg ch-5.

Rnd 12: Ch 1, sc in same st as join; * (in next ch-2 sp work sc, picot, and sc) 5 times; in next dc work sc, picot, and sc; (in next ch-2 sp work sc, picot, and sc) 5 times; sk dc, sc in next dc; rep from * around; join with sl st to sc at beg of rnd. Fasten off.

Blue-and-White-Checked Place Mats

Shown on pages 22–23.

Mats measure 13x19 inches.

MATERIALS
For two mats
Unger Roly Poly yarn (3½-ounce skein): 3 skeins of off-white, 2 skeins of bright blue
Size F aluminum crochet hook or size to obtain gauge

Abbreviations: See page 78.
Gauge: 4 bobbles = 1 inch.

INSTRUCTIONS
Note: Work these mats with two yarn colors at the same time, stitching with one color while carrying the second color along the top of the work and crocheting over. Always keep the light-colored yarn toward you or at the left side of the work and the blue yarn toward the back of the work. Do not crisscross the yarn colors from front to back.

When changing yarn colors, work the bobble st to the point where 5 lps are on the hook, then drop the color in use; with the new color, complete the stitch.

With off-white, ch 72 loosely.

Row 1: Dc in third ch from hook and in each ch across—71 dc, counting turning-ch as stitch; ch 2, turn. Tie blue yarn around turning ch-2 post.

Row 2: Sk first dc; lay blue yarn along the top of the work and, with off-white, **yo, draw up lp in next dc, yo, draw up lp in same dc, yo, draw through all 5 lps on hook—bobble made;** work bobble in each of next 2 dc, completing the bobble with blue.

* With blue, work bobble in each of next 3 dc, changing to off-white at end of third bobble; with white, work bobble in each of next 3 dc, changing to blue at end of third bobble; rep from * across row, ending with 3 off-white bobbles in last 3 dc, dc in top of turning ch-2; ch 2, turn.

Row 3: Sk first dc, * work off-white bobble in each of next 3 dc, blue bobble in each of next 3 dc; rep from * across; end with 3 off-white bobbles in last 3 dc, dc in top of turning-ch to point where 2 lps rem on hook; with blue, yo and complete stitch; ch 2, turn.

Row 4: Sk first dc, * work blue bobble in each of next 3 dc, work off-white bobble in each of next 3 dc; rep from * across, ending with 3 blue bobbles in last 3 dc, dc in top of ch-2; ch 2, turn.

Row 5: Rep Row 4; change to off-white at end of row; ch 2, turn.

Rep rows 2–5 until 17 blocks are completed; fasten off.

EDGING: Join off-white yarn in any corner st, ch 3, work 2 dc in same st. Dc evenly spaced around mat, working 3 dc in each corner. Work approximately 70 dc across both long edges and 56 dc across both short edges; join with sl st to top of beg ch-3. Fasten off.

Diagonal-Furrows Place Mat

Shown on page 24.

Mat measures 16x18 inches.

MATERIALS
Lily 18th-Century Bedspread Cotton (500-yard skein): 1 skein ecru
Size 7 steel crochet hook or size to obtain gauge

Abbreviations: See page 78.
Gauge: 9 dc = 1 inch; 4 rows = 1 inch.

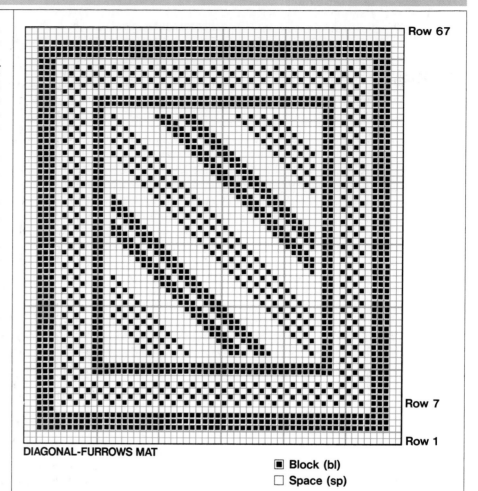

DIAGONAL-FURROWS MAT

■ Block (bl)
□ Space (sp)

Row 67

Row 7

Row 1

INSTRUCTIONS
Beg on a long edge, ch 188.

Row 1: Dc in eighth ch from hook; * **ch 2, sk 2 ch, dc in next ch—sp made;** rep from * across row—61 sp; ch 5, turn.

Row 2: Sk first dc, dc in next dc, * ch 2, dc in next dc; rep from * across to last sp; ch 2, sk 2 ch of turning-ch, dc in next ch; ch 5, turn—61 sp.

Row 3: Sk first dc, dc in next dc, ch 2, dc in next dc; * **2 dc in next ch-2 sp, dc in next dc—bl made;** rep from * across to last 2 sp; ch 2, dc in next dc, ch 2, sk 2 ch of turning-ch, dc in next ch; ch 5, turn.

Rows 4–5: Sk first dc, dc in next dc, ch 2, dc in each dc across row to last 2 sp—57 bl; ch 2, dc in next dc, ch 2, sk 2 ch of turning-ch, dc in next ch; ch 5, turn.

Row 6: Sk first dc, dc in next dc, ch 2, dc in next 10 dc; * **ch 2, sk 2 dc, dc in next dc—sp over bl made;** work 50 more sp; dc in next 9 dc; ch 2, dc in next dc, ch 2, sk 2 ch, dc in next ch; ch 5, turn.

Rows 7–67: Work from chart, *above.* Read all even-numbered rows from left to right and odd-numbered rows from right to left. Begin all even-numbered rows as indicated at the beginning of Row 2 up to the *. End all odd-numbered rows as indicated at the end of Row 3 following the *.

Ch 1, turn at end of Row 67.

EDGING: Working along the long edge of the mat, in first sp work 3 sc, * 3 sc in next sp, **ch 4, sl st in last sc made—picot made;** 3 sc in next sp; rep from * to corner sp; in corner sp work 3 sc, picot, and 3 sc; rep from first * to complete next side and corner; work rem two sides to correspond. Work 3 sc and picot in same sp as first sp to complete corner; join to first sc; fasten off.

Filet Dessert Mat

Shown on page 25.

Mat measures 9x13 inches.

MATERIALS

Lily 18th-Century Bedspread
  Cotton (500-yard skein): 1
  skein of off-white
Size 7 steel crochet hook or size
  to obtain gauge

Abbreviations: See page 78.
Gauge: 9 dc = 1 inch; 4 rows = 1
inch.

INSTRUCTIONS

Beg along a long edge, ch 128.
Row 1: Dc in eighth ch from
hook, *** ch 2, sk 2 ch, dc in next
ch—sp made;** rep from * across
row—41 sp; ch 5, turn.
Row 2: Sk first dc, dc in next dc;
*** 2 dc in next ch-2 sp, dc in next
dc—bl made;** ch 2, dc in next dc;
rep from * across row; end ch 2,
sk 2 ch, dc in next ch; ch 5, turn.
Row 3: Sk first dc, dc in next dc,
*** ch 2, sk 2 dc, dc in next dc—sp
over bl made;** work 1 bl; rep from
* across row; end ch 2, sk 2 ch, dc
in next ch; ch 5, turn.
Rows 4–34: Work from chart,
below. Read all even-numbered

rows from left to right and odd-
numbered rows from right to left.
End each row with *ch 5, turn.* Beg
each row with *sk first dc, dc in
next dc.* At end of Row 34, ch 1.

EDGING: Working along the
long edge of the mat, in first sp
work 3 sc, * 3 sc in next sp, **ch 4,
sl st in last sc made—picot
made;** 3 sc in next sp; rep from *
to corner sp; in corner sp work 3
sc, picot, and 3 sc; rep from first *
to complete next side and corner;
work rem 2 sides to correspond.
Work 3 sc and picot in same sp as
first sp to complete corner; join to
first sc; fasten off.

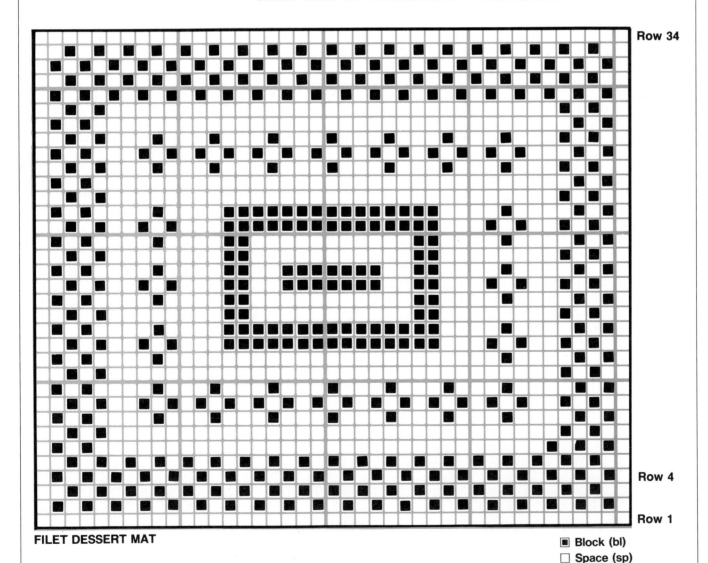

Row 34

Row 4

Row 1

FILET DESSERT MAT

■ Block (bl)
□ Space (sp)

Lacy Place Mat

Shown on page 26.

Mat measures 14x20 inches.

MATERIALS
J. & P. Coats Knit-Cro-Sheen
(250-yard ball): 3 balls of
white
Size 9 steel crochet hook

Abbreviations: See page 78.
Gauge: One block is 6 inches
square.

INSTRUCTIONS
BLOCK 1: Beg in center, ch 9,
join with sl st to form ring.

Rnd 1: Work 16 sc in ring; join
with sl st to sc at beg of rnd.

Rnd 2: Ch 7, trc in next 2 sc, ch
3, * trc in next 2 sc, ch 3; rep from
* 5 times more; end trc in last sc;
join with sl st in fourth ch of beg
ch-7—8 ch-3 sp.

Rnd 3: Sl st into next ch-3 sp,
**ch 4, in same sp work 2 trc, ch 3,
and 3 trc—beg shell made;** * 8 trc
in next ch-3 sp, in next ch-3 sp
work **3 trc, ch 3, and 3 trc—shell
made;** rep from * around; end 8
trc in last ch-3 sp; join with sl st
in top of beg ch-4.

Rnd 4: Sl st in next 2 trc and
into ch-sp, work beg shell; * ch 3,
2 trc in first trc of 8-trc grp, trc in
next 6 trc, 2 trc in next trc; ch 3,
shell in ch-3 sp of shell; rep from *
2 times more; ch 3, 2 trc in first
trc of 8-trc grp, trc in next 6 trc, 2
trc in next trc, ch 3, join in top of
beg ch-4.

Rnd 5: Sl st in next 2 trc and
into ch-sp, work beg shell, * ch 4,
trc in each of first 2 trc of 10-trc
grp, dc in next 2 trc, sc in next trc,
ch 3, sc in next trc, dc in next 2
trc, trc in next 2 trc; ch 4, shell in
ch-sp of shell; rep from * around;
end ch 4, join in top of beg ch-4.

Rnd 6: Sl st in next 2 trc and
into ch-sp, work beg shell; ch 3, in
same sp work 3 trc; * ch 5, sk 3
trc of shell, trc in next trc, ch 3, in
next ch-3 sp work **trc, ch 3, and
trc—V st made;** ch 3, sk 4 sts, trc
in next trc; ch 5, in ch-3 sp of next
shell work (3 trc, ch 3) 2 times
and 3 trc; rep from * around; end
ch 5, join in top of beg ch-4.

Rnd 7: Sl st in next 2 trc and
into ch-sp, work beg shell; * ch
10, shell in next ch-3 sp; ch 5, sk
3 trc of shell, trc in next trc, ch 3,
(V st in next trc) 2 times; ch 3, trc
in next trc, ch 5; shell in ch-3 sp
of next shell; rep from * around;
end ch 5, join in top of beg ch-4.

Rnd 8: Sl st in next 2 trc and
into ch-sp, work beg shell; * ch 5,
in ch-10 lp work sc, ch 4, and sc;
ch 5, shell in ch-3 sp of next shell;
ch 5, sk 3 trc of shell, trc in next
trc, V st in next trc, sk trc, (V st in
next trc) 2 times; trc in next trc,
ch 5, shell in ch-3 sp of next shell;
rep from * around; end ch 5, join
in top of beg ch-4.

Rnd 9: Sl st in next 2 trc and
into ch-sp, work beg shell; * ch 5,
in ch-4 lp work 9 trc, ch 5, shell in
ch-3 sp of next shell. Ch 5, sc in
ch-5 lp, (ch 5, sc in ch-3 sp of V st)
3 times, ch 5, sc in next ch-5 lp,
ch 5, shell in ch-3 sp of next shell;
rep from * around; end ch 5, join
in top of beg ch-4; fasten off.

ASSEMBLING OF BLOCKS:
Follow instructions for the first 8
rnds for all the remaining blocks.
Rnd 9, *below,* is the connecting
rnd for blocks 2-6. Blocks 1–4
connect on only one side. Blocks
5–6 connect on two sides.

BLOCK 2: Work rnds 1–8 of
Block 1. Work Rnd 9, *below,* to
join the two blocks.

Rnd 9: Sl st in next 2 trc and
into ch-sp, work beg shell; * ch 5,
in ch-4 lp work 9 trc, drop hook
from work and draw lp through
ninth trc of connecting block, ch
5, 3 trc in ch-3 sp of next shell of
block in progress; ch 2, drop hook
from work and draw lp through
the ch-3 lp of shell on connecting
block, ch 2, 3 trc in same ch-3 sp
of block in progress; ch 2, drop
hook from work and draw lp
through the ch-5 lp of connecting
block, ch 3, sc in next ch-5 lp of
block in progress; (ch 2, drop
hook from work and draw the lp
through the ch-5 lp of connecting
block, ch 3, sc in ch-3 lp of V st) 3
times; ch 2, drop hook from work
and draw lp through next ch-5 lp
of connecting block, ch 3, sc in
ch-5 lp of block in progress; ch 2,
drop hook from work and draw lp

through next ch-5 lp of connecting block, ch 3, 3 trc in ch-3 sp of
block in progress; ch 2, drop hook
from work and draw lp through
ch-lp of shell on connecting
block, ch 2, 3 trc in same ch-3 sp
of block in progress. Ch 5, in ch-4
lp work 1 trc, drop hook from
work and draw lp through the
first trc of connecting block, in
same ch-4 lp work 8 more trc;
complete block following instructions for Rnd 9 of Block 1 with no
more joining. Fasten off.

Connect Block 3 to Block 2;
connect Block 4 to top of Block 1.
Connect Block 5 to blocks 2 and 4
and Block 6 to blocks 3 and 5.
When each block is connected on
the appropriate side or sides,
work the remaining sides as for
Block 1.

EDGING: Join thread in fifth
trc of the 9-trc grp in upper right
corner.

Rnd 1: Ch 1, sc in same st, ch 6,
* in ch-3 sp of next shell work 12
dtr (yo 3 times); ch 6, sk next ch-5
lp, sc in next ch-5 lp, (ch 5, sc in
next lp) 3 times, ch 6, in next
shell sp work 12 dtr, (ch 6, sc in
fifth trc of 9-trc grp) 2 times, ch 6;
rep from * 2 times more except
work instructions in last set of ( )s
once instead of 2 times; ch 6. Rep
instructions bet *s 2 times to
work next side to correspond;
Work rem two sides as established; end ch 6, sc in sc at beg of
rnd to join.

Rnd 2: Ch 6, * (dc in next dtr, ch
1) 11 times, dc in next dtr; ch 6,
sk ch-6 lp, sc in next ch-5 lp, (ch
5, sc in next ch-5 lp) 2 times; ch 6,
(dc in next dtr, ch 1) 11 times, dc
in next dtr, ch 6, sk ch-6 lp **, dc
in next ch-6 lp, ch 6, rep from * 1
time more; rep from * to the **; sc
in sc in corner, ch 6; rep from first
* to work second side following
instructions up to corner; ch 6, sc
in sc in corner; work rem two
sides to correspond; end ch 6, sc
to sc at beg of rnd to join.

Rnd 3: Ch 5, * (dc in next dc, ch
2) 11 times, dc in next dc; ch 5, sk
next ch-6 lp, sc in next ch-5 lp, ch
continued

5, sc in next ch-5 lp; ch 5, (dc in next dc, ch 2) 11 times, dc in next dc; ch 5 **, dc in next dc, ch 5; rep from * 1 time more; rep from * to the **; sc in sc in corner, ch 5; rep from first * to work second side following instructions up to corner, sc in corner; work rem two sides to correspond; end ch 5, sc in sc at beg of rnd to join.

Rnd 4: **Ch 3, sc in last sc made—picot made;** * 4 sc in next ch-5 lp, sc in next dc, **ch 3, sc in last sc made—picot made;** (2 sc in next ch-2 sp, 2 sc in next ch-2 sp, sc in next dc, picot) 5 times; 2 sc in next lp, 4 sc in next lp; 2 sc, picot, and 2 sc in next lp; 4 sc in next lp, sc in next dc, picot, (2 sc in next ch-2 lp, 2 sc in next ch-2 lp, sc in next dc, picot) 5 times; 2 sc in next lp, 4 sc in next lp **, sc in next dc, picot, 4 sc in next lp; rep from * 1 time more; rep from * to the **; sc in corner sc, work picot; rep from first * to work second side following instructions up to corner; sc in corner sc, picot; work rem 2 sides to correspond; end 4 sc in last ch-5 lp; join to base of first picot at beg of rnd. Fasten off.

Round Mat

Shown on page 27.

Mat is 15¾ inches in diameter.

MATERIALS
DMC Cebelia crochet cotton,
　　Size 10 (50-gram ball): 1 ball
　　of white
Size 7 steel crochet hook

Abbreviations: See page 78.

INSTRUCTIONS
Beg at center, ch 5, join with sl st to form ring.

Rnd 1: Ch 5, dc in ring, (ch 2, dc in ring) 6 times; ch 2, join with sl st to third ch of beg ch-5.

Rnd 2: Sl st into ch-2 lp, ch 3, 3 dc in same lp; * 4 dc in next ch-2 lp; rep from * around; join to top of beg ch-3.

Rnd 3: Ch 1, sc in same st as join; * ch 4, sk dc, sc in next dc;

rep from * 14 times more; end ch 2, join with dc in sc at beg of rnd.

Rnd 4: Ch 3, in lp just made work 3 dc, ch 1; * 4 dc in next lp, ch 1; rep from * around; end ch 1, join to top of ch-3 at beg of rnd.

Rnd 5: Ch 3, dc in next 3 dc, ch 2; * dc in next 4 dc, ch 2; rep from * around; join to top of beg ch-3.

Rnd 6: Sl st in next 3 dc; * in next ch-2 sp work sc, ch 3, and sc; ch 5; rep from * around; end ch 5, join with sl st to sc at beg of rnd. Fasten off.

Rnd 7: Join thread in any ch-5 lp, **ch 3, in same lp work dc, ch 2, and 2 dc—beg shell made;** * ch 4, in next ch-5 lp **2 dc, ch 2, 2 dc—shell made;** rep from * around; end ch 4, join to top of beg ch-3.

Rnd 8: Sl st in next dc and into ch-2 sp, work beg shell. (*Note:* Rnds 9–25 begin this way and read "sl st and work beg shell.") * Ch 5, shell in ch-2 sp of shell; rep from * around; end ch 5, join to top of beg ch-3.

Rnd 9: Sl st and work beg shell; * ch 2, dc in center ch of ch-5 lp, ch 2, shell in ch-2 sp of shell; rep from * around; end ch 2, join with sl st to top of beg ch-3. (*Note:* Rounds 10–26 end this way and read "end ch 2, join.")

Rnd 10: Sl st and work beg shell; * ch 2, sk 2 dc of shell, 3 dc in next dc, ch 2, shell in ch-2 sp of next shell; rep from * around; end ch 2, join.

Rnd 11: Sl st and work beg shell; * ch 2, 2 dc in first dc of 3-dc grp, dc in next dc, 2 dc in next dc, ch 2, shell in ch-2 sp of shell; rep from * around; end ch 2, join.

Rnd 12: Sl st and work beg shell; * ch 2, dc in each of first 2 dc of 5-dc grp, ch 2, sk dc, dc in next 2 dc, ch 2, shell in ch-2 sp of shell; rep from * around; end ch 2, join.

Rnd 13: Sl st and work beg shell; * ch 2, sk 2 dc of shell, dc in each of next 2 dc, 3 dc in ch-2 sp, dc in next 2 dc, ch 2, shell in ch-2 sp of shell; rep from * around; end ch 2, join.

Rnd 14: Sl st and work beg shell; * ch 2, dc in first 3 dc of 7-dc

grp, ch 2, sk dc, dc in next 3 dc, ch 2, shell in ch-2 sp of shell; rep from * around; end ch 2, join.

Rnd 15: Sl st and work beg shell; * ch 2, sk 2 dc of shell, dc in next 3 dc, 3 dc in ch-2 sp, dc in next 3 dc, ch 2, shell in ch-2 sp of shell; rep from * around; end ch 2, join.

Rnd 16: Sl st and work beg shell; * ch 2, dc in first 4 dc of 9-dc grp, ch 2, sk dc, dc in next 4 dc, ch 2, shell in ch-2 sp of shell; rep from * around; end ch 2, join.

Rnd 17: Sl st and work beg shell; * ch 2, sk 2 dc of shell, dc in next 4 dc, 3 dc in ch-2 lp, dc in next 4 dc, ch 2, shell in ch-2 sp of next shell; rep from * around; end ch 2, join.

Rnd 18: Sl st and work beg shell; * ch 2, sk 2 dc of shell, (dc in next 3 dc, ch 1, sk dc) 2 times, dc in next 3 dc, ch 2, shell in ch-2 sp of next shell; rep from * around; end ch 2, join.

Rnd 19: Sl st and work beg shell; * ch 2, sk 2 dc of shell, dc in next 3 dc, 2 dc in ch-1 sp, ch 3, sk 3 dc, 2 dc in next ch-1 sp, dc in next 3 dc, ch 2, shell in ch-2 sp of next shell; rep from * around; end ch 2, join.

Rnd 20: Sl st and work beg shell; * ch 2, dc in first 3 dc of 5-dc grp, ch 2, sk dc, dc in next dc, 3 dc in ch-3 sp, dc in next dc, ch 2, sk dc, dc in next 3 dc, ch 2, shell in ch-2 sp of next shell; rep from * around; end ch 2, join.

Rnd 21: Sl st and work beg shell; * ch 2, sk 2 dc of shell, dc in next 3 dc, ch 2, dc in next dc, ch 3, sk 3 dc, dc in next dc, ch 2, dc in next 3 dc, ch 2, shell in ch-2 sp of next shell; rep from * around; end ch 2, join.

Rnd 22: Sl st and work beg shell; * ch 2, sk 2 dc of shell, dc in next 3 dc, ch 2, dc in next dc, 4 dc in ch-3 lp, dc in dc, ch 2, dc in next 3 dc, ch 2, shell in ch-2 sp of next shell; rep from * around; end ch 2, join.

Rnd 23: Sl st and work beg shell; * ch 2, sk 2 dc of shell, dc in next 3 dc, 2 dc in ch-2 sp, dc in next 2 dc, ch 3, sk 2 dc, dc in next

2 dc, 2 dc in next ch-2 sp, dc in next 3 dc, ch 2, shell in ch-2 sp of next shell; rep from * around; end ch 2, join.

Rnd 24: Sl st and work beg shell; * ch 2, sk 2 dc of shell, dc in next 3 dc, ch 2, sk 2 dc, dc in next 2 dc, 4 dc in ch-3 sp, dc in next 2 dc, ch 2, sk 2 dc, dc in next 3 dc, ch 2, shell in ch-2 sp of next shell; rep from * around; end ch 2, join.

Rnd 25: Sl st and work beg shell; * ch 2, sk 2 dc of shell, dc in next 3 dc, ch 2, dc in next dc, ch 2, sk dc, dc in next dc, ch 3, sk 2 dc, dc in next dc, ch 2, sk dc, dc in next dc, ch 2, dc in next 3 dc, ch 2, shell in ch-2 sp of next shell; rep from * around; end ch 2, join.

Note: To work trc-cl in next three rounds, work as follows: **Holding back last lp of each trc, work 2 trc in sp or st, then yo and draw through all 3 lps on hook—trc-cl made.**

Rnd 26: Sl st in next dc and into ch-2 sp, ch 3, in same sp work 5 dc; * ch 2, sk 2 dc of shell, sc in next 3 dc, ch 3, sk 2 ch-2 lps; in ch-3 lp work (trc-cl, ch 2) 2 times and trc-cl; ch 3, sk 2 ch-sp, sc in next 3 dc, ch 2, 6 dc in ch-2 sp of next shell; rep from * around; end ch 2, join.

Rnd 27: Sc in next dc, * (ch 3, sk dc, sc in next dc) 2 times; ch 3, sc in center sc of 3-sc grp, ch 4, trc-cl in first cl, ch 2; in next trc-cl work (trc-cl, ch 2) 2 times and trc-cl; ch 2, trc-cl in next trc-cl; ch 4, sc in center sc of 3-sc grp; ch 3, sk first dc of dc-grp, sc in next dc; rep from * around; end ch 3, join to first sc.

Rnd 28: Sl st in next ch of ch-3 lp, sc in same lp; ch 3, sc in next lp, ch 3, * (in top of next cl work trc-cl, ch 2, and trc-cl; ch 2) 4 times; in top of next cl work trc-cl, ch 2, and trc-cl; ch 3, sk next 2 lps, sc in next lp, ch 3, sc in next lp, ch 3; rep from * around; end ch 3, join to sc at beg of rnd.

Rnd 29: Sl st into ch-3 lp, ch 1, sc in same lp; **ch 3, sc in third ch from hook—picot made;** sc in same lp; * 4 sc in next lp; (in next ch-2 sp work sc, picot, and sc) 9 times, 4 sc in next lp, in next lp work sc, picot, and sc; rep from * around; join with sl st to beg sc. Fasten off.

Hexagon-Motif Tablecloth

Shown on pages 28–29.

Cloth shown measures 62x80 inches. See note *below.*

MATERIALS
DMC Cebelia crochet cotton, Size 20 (405-yard ball): 1 ball makes 24 motifs (19 balls for size cloth shown)
Size 8 steel crochet hook or size to obtain gauge

Abbreviations: See page 78.
Gauge: One motif measures 3½ inches from point to point.

INSTRUCTIONS
Note: The cloth shown consists of 454 motifs. Work the first motif through Rnd 7. Work all other motifs through Rnd 6, then join to the succeeding motif on Rnd 7. When all motifs are made, the cloth is completely assembled.

You easily can adjust this pattern to fit any size table. Work four motifs and connect them as you make them. From your swatch, determine the gauge and number of motifs required to fit your table.

The symbol ** in these instructions indicates where the last repeat in the round ends. The symbol does not designate pattern repeats within the rounds.

FIRST MOTIF: Ch 6, join with sl st to form ring.

Rnd 1: Ch 3, work 23 dc in ring; join with sl st to top of beg ch-3.

Rnd 2: Ch 4, dc in next dc; * ch 1, dc in next dc; rep from * around; end ch 1, join with sl st to third ch of beg ch-4—24 ch-1 sp.

Rnd 3: Sl st into ch-1 sp, sc in same sp; * ch 4, sc in next ch-1 sp; rep from * around; end ch 4, join with sl st in sc at beg of rnd—24 ch-4 lps.

Rnd 4: Sl st in next 2 ch of ch-4 lp, sc in same lp; * ch 4, sc in next ch-4 lp; rep from * around; end ch 4, join with sl st in sc at beg of rnd.

Rnd 5: Sl st into next ch-4 lp, ch 3, 2 dc in same lp, * ch 3, 3 dc in next lp, ch 3, sc in next lp, ch 4, sc in next lp **, ch 3, 3 dc in next lp; rep from * around, ending at ** on last rep; ch 3, join with sl st to top of beg ch-3.

Rnd 6: Ch 3, dc in next 2 dc; * in ch-3 lp work 4 dc, ch 2, and 4 dc; dc in next 3 dc, ch 3, sk next lp, sc in ch-4 lp **, ch 3, dc in next 3 dc; rep from * around, ending at ** on last rep; ch 3, join with sl st to top of beg ch-3.

Rnd 7: Ch 3, dc in next 4 dc, **ch 6, sl st in last dc made—picot made;** dc in next 2 dc; * in ch-2 sp work 3 dc, ch 3, and 3 dc; dc in next 2 dc, picot, dc in next 5 dc, picot **, dc in next 5 dc, picot, dc in next 2 dc; rep from * around, ending at ** on last rep; join with sl st to top of beg ch-3. Fasten off.

SECOND MOTIF: Work as First Motif through Rnd 6. Then begin to work Rnd 7 as follows: Ch 3, dc in next 4 dc, picot, dc in next 2 dc; *** in ch-2 sp work 3 dc, ch 2, drop hook from work and insert hook in the corner ch-3 sp of the previous motif, draw the dropped lp through, ch 2, work 3 dc in same ch-2 sp on motif in progress—corner join made.** Dc in next 2 dc, **ch 3, drop hook from work, insert hook in the corresponding picot of connecting motif, draw the dropped lp through, ch 3, sl st in last dc made of motif in progress—picot join made;** dc in next 5 dc, work a picot join, dc in next 5 dc, work a picot join, dc in next 2 dc; work a corner join in next ch-2 sp. Work remaining five sides as for Rnd 7 of First Motif with no more joinings.

Join 22 more motifs (a total of 24) to complete the first lengthwise row. Refer to the diagram on page 38 to assemble the hexagon motifs for the tablecloth as shown in the photo on pages 28–29.

continued

The second row consists of 25 motifs. The first and last motifs of the row extend beyond the first row. The second motif of this row has three sides that join to the cloth; work the joinings as already established. Complete the remaining three sides with no more joinings.

Row 3 consists of 26 motifs; the first and last motifs of this row extend beyond the second row.

Row 4 consists of 27 motifs; the first and last motifs of this row extend beyond the third row.

Row 5 consists of 26 motifs; the motifs are in the same position as Row 3 and begin the scalloped edging.

Row 6 consists of 27 motifs; the motifs are in the same position as Row 4.

Repeat rows 5 and 6 eight times more. Then assemble the remaining three rows to mirror rows 3, 2, and 1.

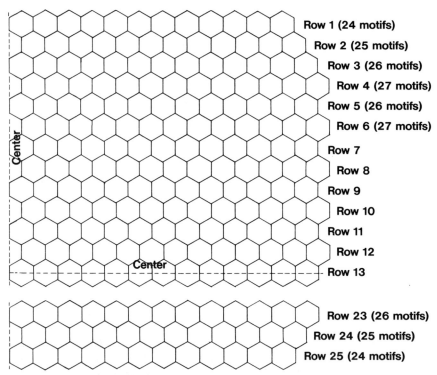

ASSEMBLY DIAGRAM FOR HEXAGON-MOTIF TABLECLOTH

Runner

Shown on page 30.

Runner measures 16x62 inches.

MATERIALS
J. & P. Coats crochet cotton, Size 10 (350-yard ball): 3 balls of ecru or white
Size 7 steel crochet hook or size to obtain gauge

Abbreviations: See page 78.
Gauge: One block measures 4½ inches square.

INSTRUCTIONS
Note: The symbol ** in these instructions indicates where the last repeat in the row ends. The symbol does not designate pattern repeats within the rounds.

The table runner shown consists of 52 motifs joined in 13 rows, each row containing four motifs. Use this motif to make any size runner or centerpiece, or even a tablecloth.

FIRST MOTIF: Ch 8, join with sl st to form ring.

Rnd 1: Ch 4, 2 trc in ring; (ch 2, 3 trc in ring) 7 times; end ch 2, join with sl st to top of beg ch-4—8 ch-2 sp.

Rnd 2: Sl st in next 2 trc and into ch-2 sp, ch 4, 4 trc in same sp, (ch 2, 4 dc in next ch-2 sp, ch 2, 5 trc in next ch-2 sp) 3 times; ch 2, 4 dc in last ch-2 sp, ch 2; join to top of beg ch-4.

Rnd 3: Ch 1, sc in same st as join, sc in next 4 trc, * ch 2, dc in next dc, dc bet first and second dc of 4-dc grp, dc in next dc, ch 2, dc in next dc, dc bet third and fourth dc of 4-dc grp, dc in next dc **; ch 2, sc in next 5 trc; rep from * around, ending at ** on last rep; ch 2, join to sc at beg of rnd.

Rnd 4: Ch 1, sc in same st as join, * (ch 3, sc in next sc) 4 times, ch 2, dc in next 3 dc, ch 3, dc in next 3 dc **; ch 2, sc in next sc; rep from * around, ending at ** on last rep; ch 2, join with sl st to sc at beg of rnd.

Rnd 5: Sl st in next 2 ch of ch-3 lp, ch 1, sc in same lp; * (ch 3, sc in next lp) 3 times; ch 2, dc in next 3 dc; ch 1, in ch-3 lp work (dc, ch 1) 3 times and dc; ch 1, dc in next 3 dc **; ch 2, sc in next ch-3 lp; rep from * around, ending at ** on last rep; ch 2, join with sl st to sc at beg of rnd.

Rnd 6: Sl st in next 2 ch of ch-3 lp, ch 1, sc in same lp; * (ch 3, sc in next lp) 2 times; ch 2, dc in next 3 dc; ch 1, (dc in next ch-1 sp, ch 1) 2 times; in next ch-1 sp work dc, ch 2, and dc; ch 1, (dc in next ch-1 sp, ch 1) 2 times, dc in next 3 dc **; ch 2, sc in next ch-3 lp; rep from * around, ending at ** on last rep; ch 2, join to beg sc.

Rnd 7: Sl st in next 2 ch of ch-3 lp, ch 1, sc in same lp; * ch 3, sc in next ch-3 lp, ch 2, dc in next 3 dc; (ch 1, dc in next ch-1 lp) 3 times, ch 1, in next ch-2 sp work 4 dc; (ch 1, dc in next ch-1 lp) 3 times, ch 1, dc in next 3 dc **; ch 2, sc in next ch-3 lp; rep from * around, ending at ** on last rep; ch 2, join to sc at beg of rnd.

Row 1 (24 motifs)
Row 2 (25 motifs)
Row 3 (26 motifs)
Row 4 (27 motifs)
Row 5 (26 motifs)
Row 6 (27 motifs)
Row 7
Row 8
Row 9
Row 10
Row 11
Row 12
Row 13
Center
Center
Row 23 (26 motifs)
Row 24 (25 motifs)
Row 25 (24 motifs)

Rnd 8: Sl st in next 2 ch of ch-3 lp, ch 1, sc in same lp, * ch 2, dc in next 3 dc, (ch 1, dc in next ch-1 sp) 3 times, ch 1, 4 dc in next ch-1 sp, ch 5, 4 dc in next ch-1 sp, (ch 1, dc in next ch-1 sp) 3 times, ch 1, dc in next 3 dc **; ch 2, sc in ch-3 lp; rep from * around, ending at ** on last rep; ch 2, join.

Rnd 9: Sl st in next 2 ch and dc, ch 3, dc in next 2 dc, * (ch 1, dc in next ch-1 sp) 4 times; ch 1, in ch-5 lp work (3 trc, ch 1) 3 times and 3 trc—4-trc grp in ch-5 lp; (ch 1, dc in next ch-1 sp) 4 times, ch 1, dc in next 3 dc **; sk next 2 lp, dc in next 3 dc; rep from * around, ending at ** on last rep; join with sl st to top of beg ch-3.

Rnd 10: Ch 1, sc in same st as join; ch 3, * **(in next ch-1 sp work 2 dc, ch 4, sl st in last dc made, and 2 dc—picot shell made;** ch 2, sc in next ch-1 sp, ch 2) 6 times; in next ch-1 sp work picot shell **; ch 3, sc in sp bet 3-dc grp, ch 3; rep from * around, ending at ** on last rep; ch 3, join to first sc.

ASSEMBLING THE BLOCKS: Follow the instructions for the first 9 rnds for all rem blocks. Rnd 10, *below,* is the connecting rnd for blocks 2–52.

SECOND MOTIF: Work rnds 1–9 of First Motif. Work Rnd 10 as follows to join two blocks.

Rnd 10: Ch 1, sc in same st as join, ch 3, * (in next ch-1 sp work picot shell, ch 2, sc in next ch-1 sp, ch 2) 3 times; **in next ch-1 sp work 2 dc, ch 2, drop hook from work, insert hook in corresponding picot lp of connecting block and draw the dropped lp through, ch 2, sl st in last dc of block in progress, in same sp work 2 dc to complete picot shell—2 picot shells joined.**
Continue to work side as established and join the motif in progress to its connecting block as you work the picot shells. Join all picot shells on side and next corner; work rem sides as established for Rnd 10 of First Motif without joining. Work rem blocks as established for Second Motif.

Cluny-Lace, Hexagon-Motif Tablecloth

Shown on page 31.

Cloth measures 53x68 inches.

MATERIALS
DMC Baroque crochet cotton (400-yard skein): 13 skeins of ecru or white (1 skein makes 15 motifs)
Quilting or sewing thread to match crochet cotton
Size 8 steel crochet hook or size to obtain gauge

Abbreviations: See page 78.
Gauge: Motif measures 5 inches in diameter across the widest points.

INSTRUCTIONS
MOTIF (make 188): Beg at center, ch 5, join with sl st to form ring.
Rnd 1: Ch 1, work 12 sc in ring, join with sl st to sc at beg of rnd.
Rnd 2: Ch 1, sc in same st as join, (ch 5, sk sc, sc in next sc) 5 times; ch 5, join with sl st to beg sc—6 ch-5 lps.
Rnd 3: Sl st in next 2 ch of ch-5 lp, ch 7, sk next ch, hdc in next ch, (ch 5, hdc in second ch of next ch-5 lp, ch 5, hdc in fourth ch of same ch-5 lp) 5 times; ch 5, join with sl st in second ch of beg ch-7.
Rnd 4: Ch 3, in same st as join work 2 dc, sc in ch-5 lp, (3 dc in next hdc, sc in next ch-5 lp) 11 times; join with sl st to top of ch-3 at beg of rnd.
Rnd 5: Ch 1, sc in same st as join, sc in next 2 dc, 2 sc in next sc; * sc in next 3 dc, 2 sc in next sc; rep from * around; end 2 sc in last sc; join to first sc—60 sc.
Rnd 6: Ch 1, sc in same st as join, sc in next 3 sc, 2 sc in next sc; * sc in next 4 sc, 2 sc in next sc; rep from * around; 2 sc in last sc; join to first sc—72 sc.
Rnd 7: Sl st in next sc, ch 4, 4 trc in same st as sl st; * ch 3, sk 2 sc, sc in next sc, ch 3, sk 2 sc, 5 trc in next sc; rep from * around; end

ch 3, sk 2 sc, sc in next sc, ch 3, join to top of beg ch-4.
Rnd 8: * Ch 4, **holding back last lp of each trc on hook, trc in next 4 trc, yo, draw through 5 lps on hook—cl made;** ch 4, sl st in first ch of next ch-3 lp, ch 3, sl st in third ch of same ch-3 lp; **sc in next trc, hdc in next trc, 3 dc in next trc, hdc in next trc, sc in next trc—shell made;** sl st in first ch of next ch-3 lp, ch 3, sl st in third ch of same ch-3 lp, sl st in next trc; rep from * around; join last ch-3 with sl st in last ch.
Rnd 9: Sl st in next 4 ch of first cl, sc in top of cl; * ch 8, sc in 3 dc of shell, ch 8, sc in top of next cl; rep from * around; join last ch-8 with sl st in first sc.
Rnd 10: Ch 4, in same sc as join work trc, dtr (yo 3 times), and 2 trc (dtr form the points for the hexagon); * ch 3, in sixth ch of ch-8 lp work **trc, ch 2, and trc—V st made;** in next sc work V st, sk sc, in next sc work V st, sk 2 ch of next ch-8 lp, V st in next ch, ch 3, in next sc work **2 trc, dtr, and 2 trc—large shell made;** rep from * around; end ch 3, join to top of beg ch-4. Fasten off.

ASSEMBLY: With wrong sides facing, and using the sewing or quilting thread, sew motifs together in rows. Sew seven rows with 14 motifs in each row. Sew six rows with 15 motifs in each row. Then sew rows together, alternating the shorter rows with the longer rows to form the scalloped edge. The shorter rows should be along the outside edges.

EDGING: With right side facing, join thread in first trc of the second shell group of any corner motif, sc in same st, sc in next st, **ch 3, sl st in third ch from hook—picot made;** sc in next 3 sts, 3 sc in next lp, 2 sc in next ch-2 lp, sc bet V sts, picot, 2 sc in next ch-2 lp, sc bet V sts, picot, 2 sc in next ch-2 lp, sc bet V st, 2 sc in next ch-2 lp, 3 sc in next ch-3 lp, sc in next 3 sts, picot; continue to work sc and picots as established. If necessary, inc the number of sc in the ch-lps to keep work lying flat.

GIFTS FOR BABIES

As endearing as a baby's sweet thoughtfulness—that describes the combination of white with soft or bright pastels you'll find in most of the designs in this chapter. These crocheted blankets, garments, and teddy bears (they're crafted in white to look like polar bears!) are fun to stitch and sure to please baby's parents, too. Directions begin on page 48.

You'll get lots of attention when you take baby out in the ribbon-and-shell sweater, cap, and carriage blanket, *left* and *below.*

Rows of half double crochet stitches, along with beading rows, make up the center of the afghan and the yoke and sleeves on the baby sweater. When the afghan and sweater are finished, thread narrow ribbons through the beading, and tack tiny ribbon roses on the sweater and cap.

Stitch the sweater bodice, cap, and blanket border in row upon row of lacy shell stitches set off with raised treble crochet stitches.

The sweater and cap fit infants size 6 to 9 months. The blanket measures 40x45 inches.

GIFTS FOR BABIES

Delicate and feminine, the crocheted sweater and bonnet, *left* and *above,* feature smockinglike embroidery. Work the sweater and cap in shell stitches, except stitch the yoke and hat front in single crochet. Embroider the simple design on the front of the sweater and along the front edge of the cap using straight stitches and French knots.

Pint-size aviators and other adventurous kids will look dashing in the V-necked, double-breasted jacket, *opposite,* and matching cap (see inset, *opposite*). A white stripe on just one sleeve lifts this design out of the ordinary and into the heady atmosphere of sporty fashion for tots.

Both outfits can be sized for 6-, 12-, and 18-month-old children.

P laytime is the right time for a lightweight, sherbet-colored cardigan trimmed in white. The design, *opposite* and *above*, features patch pockets bordered with ribbing. Ribbing around the neckline forms a stand-up collar.

The sweater is sized for 6-, 12-, and 18-month-old kids.

The cuddly mama and baby polar bears, *opposite, left,* and *above,* are sure to be a hit with children of all ages. Crochet both bears from the same pattern, simply changing the size of the yarn.

Baby bear is 9 inches tall and wears a playsuit edged with ruffles. Mama bear is 12 inches tall; she wears a dress embellished (and shaped) with a smocked bodice.

Everything's coming up roses on the lovely Irish-crochet pillow and afghan, *above* and *opposite*. Each flower is crafted with three rows of petals and set into a 3½-inch square of airy chain loops.

The rose blocks are set between diagonally crocheted, densely textured squares and triangles that are worked separately. A shell-stitch border, with picots along the edge, completes the afghan.

If you've been eager to try your hand at Irish crochet, but been hesitant about working flowers in the fine thread most patterns call for, you'll find this design a delight. Both the afghan and pillow are crocheted using DMC Cotonia, a soft, sportweight-like yarn.

The pillow, with five rose motifs, measures 12 inches square. The afghan, with 66 rose blocks, measures 36x47 inches.

Ribbon-and-Shell Baby Sweater And Cap

Shown on pages 40–41.

Fits infant size 6 to 9 months.

MATERIALS
Susan Bates Patons baby yarn (50-gram ball): 3 balls of white
Sizes B, C, and D aluminum crochet hooks
1 package of Offray pink ribbon roses
2½ yards of ¼-inch-wide pink satin ribbon

Abbreviations: See page 78.
Gauge: 3 shells = 3 inches; 5 rows of shells = 2 inches.

INSTRUCTIONS
Note: Ch 2 at beg of row always counts as first hdc of row.

For the sweater
YOKE: Work sweater yoke from outside edge of one sleeve, across the bodice, to outside edge of other sleeve.

With Size C hook, ch 56.

Row 1: Hdc in third ch from hook and in each ch across row—55 hdc, counting turning-ch as hdc.

Row 2: Ch 4 (counts as dc and ch-1 sp), turn. Sk first 2 hdc, dc in next hdc; * ch 1, sk hdc, dc in next hdc; rep from * across; end ch 1, hdc in top of turning ch-2—27 ch-1 sp.

Row 3: Ch 2, turn. Sk first hdc, * hdc in next ch-1 sp, hdc in next dc; rep from * across; end hdc in turning ch-lp, hdc in third ch of turning ch-4 lp—55 hdc.

Rows 4–9: Ch 2, turn. Hdc in each hdc across row.

Rows 10–49: Rep rows 2–9 five times more.

Row 50: Ch 4 (counts as dc and ch-1 sp), turn. Sk first 2 hdc, dc in next hdc; (ch 1, sk hdc, dc in next hdc) 12 times (mark last stitch made for beg of right front).

Row 51 (beg back of neck): Ch 2, turn. Sk first hdc; * hdc in next ch-1 sp, hdc in next dc; rep from * across; end hdc in turning ch-lp, hdc in third ch of turning ch-4 lp—27 hdc.

Rows 52–57: Ch 2, turn; hdc in each hdc across.

Rows 58–65: Rep rows 50–57; fasten off.

RIGHT FRONT: Sk next hdc at end of Row 50, join yarn in next hdc.

Row 1: Ch 4 (counts as dc and ch-1 sp); (sk next hdc, dc in next hdc, ch 1) 12 times, dc in last hdc.

Row 2: Ch 2, turn. (Hdc in next ch-1 sp, hdc in next dc) 11 times; **yo hook, draw up lp in next sp, yo hook, draw up lp in next dc, yo hook, draw yarn through all lps on hook—hdc-dec made.**

Row 3: Ch 2, turn. Work hdc-dec over next 2 hdc; hdc in each hdc across row and top of ch-2.

Row 4: Ch 2, turn. Work hdc in each hdc across row until 3 sts rem; work hdc-dec over next 2 hdc, hdc in top of ch-2.

Rows 5–8: Rep rows 3–4 two times more.

Row 9: Rep Row 3.

Row 10: Ch 4 (counts as dc and ch-1 sp), turn. (Sk next hdc, dc in next hdc, ch 1) 7 times; dc in top of ch-2—8 sp.

Row 11: Ch 2, turn. Hdc-dec over next ch-1 sp and dc; hdc in each ch-1 sp and dc across row; end hdc in ch-4 lp, hdc in third ch of turning lp—16 sts; fasten off.

LEFT FRONT: Beg at center front edge, ch 17.

Row 1: 2 hdc in third ch from hook, hdc in each ch across—17 hdc, counting turning-ch as st.

Row 2: Ch 4, turn. Sk 2 hdc, dc in next hdc; (ch 1, sk hdc, dc in next hdc) 6 times, ch 1, sk dc, 2 dc in top of turning-ch—8 ch-1 sps.

Row 3: Ch 2, turn; 2 hdc in next dc, (hdc in next sp, hdc in next dc) 7 times; hdc in turning-lp, hdc in third ch of ch-4—19 hdc.

Row 4: Ch 2, turn; hdc in each st across; 2 hdc in top of turning-ch —20 hdc.

Row 5: Ch 2, turn; hdc in first hdc and in each hdc across row—21 hdc.

Row 6: Rep Row 4—22 hdc.

Row 7: Rep Row 5—23 hdc.

Row 8: Rep Row 4—24 hdc.

Row 9: Rep Row 5—25 hdc.

Row 10: Ch 4, turn, sk 2 hdc, dc in next hdc; (ch 1, sk next hdc, dc in next hdc) 10 times; ch 1, dc in top of turning-ch—12 ch-1 sp; ch 1, dc in same st as last dc, ch 1; do not turn.

Beg to attach neck-edge front to neck-edge back by working dc in first st of yoke. Continue in pat st across entire left side of yoke until left sleeve corresponds with right sleeve; fasten off.

Fold fronts over at shoulder seam and sew sleeve underarm seams from cuff to two rows beyond the fourth beading st pat.

BODICE: Turn yoke upside down and work as follows with C hook: *Row 1* (wrong side): Join yarn at left front edge; work 1 row of sc across to right front edge; work 31 sc across each front section and 59 sc across back.

Row 2: With D hook, ch 3, turn. * Sk sc, in next sc work **3 dc, ch 2, and 3 dc—shell made;** sk sc, dc in next sc; rep from * across—8 shells on each front and 14 shells across back.

Row 3: Ch 4, turn. * Shell in ch-2 sp of next shell, sk 2 dc of shell, trc around post of next dc *from the back;* rep from * across; end shell in shell, ch 1, dc in turning-lp.

Row 4: Ch 4, turn. * Shell in ch-2 sp of shell, trc around post of trc *from the front;* rep from * across; end shell in shell, ch 1, dc in turning ch-lp.

Rows 5–16: Rep rows 3–4 six times more—15 shell rows.

Row 17: Ch 1, turn; work 1 row of reverse sc (work from left to right) across, working sc in each st and 2 sc in each sp; fasten off.

FINISHING: With C hook, work one round of reverse sc around each sleeve edge. Join yarn at lower front edge of left side of yoke (just above the bodice); work one row of reverse sc around the left yoke front, around the neck, and down the right front to the beg of bodice; fasten off.

Cut two ribbons, each 12 inches long, and thread through the first rows of beading at the sleeve edges. Draw up to fit wrist and tie in bow. Cut two ribbons each 18 inches long and thread through beading rows at the yoke center fronts. Tie ends of ribbons in bows. Weave ribbons through two beading rows on each yoke front and back; tack ribbon ends in place. Sew four ribbon bows to front of sweater.

For the cap

BACK: With C hook, ch 32.

Row 1: Work hdc in third ch from hook and in each ch across row—31 hdc, counting turning-ch as hdc.

Row 2: Ch 4 (counts as dc and ch-1 sp), turn. Sk first 2 hdc, dc in next hdc; * ch 1, sk hdc, dc in next hdc; rep from * across; end ch 1, hdc in top of turning ch-2—15 ch-1 sp.

Row 3: Ch 2, turn. Sk first hdc, * hdc in next ch-1 sp, hdc in next dc; rep from * across; end hdc in turning ch-lp, hdc in third ch of turning ch-4 lp.

Rows 4–9: Ch 2, turn. Hdc in each hdc across row.

Rows 10–17: Rep rows 2–9.

Next 2 rows: Rep rows 2–3; fasten off at end of Row 19.

CAP FRONT: *Row 1:* Attach yarn at beg of last row of cap back. Work 28 sc up row, work 2 sc in last st; work 30 sc across top of cap back, work 2 sc in first ch of next side; work 28 sc down beg ch—90 sc.

Row 2: Ch 4, turn. * Sk 2 sc, in next sc work **3 dc, ch 2, and 3 dc—shell made;** sk 2 sc, dc in next sc; rep from * across—15 shells.

Row 3: Ch 4, turn. * Shell in ch-2 sp of next shell, sk 2 dc of shell, trc around post of next dc *from the back;* rep from * across; end shell in shell, ch 1, dc in turning-lp.

Row 4: Ch 4, turn. * Shell in ch-2 sp of shell, trc around post of trc *from the front;* rep from * across; end shell in shell, ch 1, dc in turning ch-lp.

Rows 5–12: Rep rows 3–4 four times more.

Row 13: Rep Row 3.

Row 14: Change to B hook and work shell pattern across.

Row 15: Work row of reverse sc across; fasten off.

With B hook, turn cap upside down and work one row of sc across neck edge, gathering in across the back piece of cap as you work; work 30 sts across each side and 21 sts across back—81 sc.

Row 2: Ch 4 (counts as dc and ch-1 sp), turn. Sk sc, dc in next sc; * ch 1, sk sc, dc in next sc; rep from * across; ch 1, turn.

Row 3: Sc in each dc and ch-1 sp across; fasten off.

Weave 24-inch length of ribbon through the beading row at neck edge and tie in bow. Sew ribbons bows in place.

Ribbon-and-Shell Baby Blanket

Shown on pages 40–41.

Blanket measures 40x45 inches.

MATERIALS
Susan Bates Patons sport yarn (50-gram ball): 11 balls of white
Size G aluminum crochet hook
3 yards each of ¼-inch-wide pink, yellow, and green satin ribbons

Abbreviations: See page 78.
Gauge: 9 hdc = 2 inches; 9 rows = 2¾ inches.

INSTRUCTIONS
CENTER RECTANGLE: Beg at bottom, ch 128.

Row 1: Hdc in third ch from hook and in each ch across row.

Row 2: Ch 4, turn. Sk first 2 hdc, dc in next st; * ch 1, sk hdc, dc in next hdc; rep from * across.

Row 3: Ch 3, turn. * Hdc in next ch-1 sp, hdc in next dc; rep from * across; end hdc in ch-4 turning lp, hdc in third ch of ch-4.

Row 4–9: Ch 2, turn. Sk first hdc, hdc in each hdc across row.

Rows 10–81: Rep rows 2–9 nine times more.

Row 82: Rep Row 2.

Row 83: Rep Row 3; fasten off.

Work 101 sc across each short end of rectangle.

BORDER: *Rnd 1:* Join yarn in any corner st, **ch 3, in same st work 2 dc, ch 2, and 3 dc—beg shell made;** * sk 2 sts, dc in next st, sk 2 sts, in next st work **3 dc, ch 2, and 3 dc—shell made;** rep from * around, taking care to have a shell in each corner and a dc on each side; join to top of ch-3.

Rnd 2: Sl st to ch-2 sp of beg shell; **work a beg shell in same sp, ch 2, in same sp work 3 dc—beg corner made;** * trc around post of next dc *from the front,* shell in ch-2 sp of next shell; rep from * to next corner shell; **in ch-2 sp of corner shell work (3 dc, ch 2) 2 times and 3 dc—corner made;** rep from first * to work next side. Work all rem corners and sides as established; join to top of beg ch-3.

Rnd 3: Sl st to next ch-2 sp, work a beg shell in same sp; trc around post of center dc of next 3-dc grp, shell in ch-2 sp of next shell; * trc around post of next trc, shell in ch-2 sp of next shell; rep from * to first ch-2 sp of first corner shell; work shell in this ch-2 sp, trc around post of center dc of next 3-dc grp, shell in ch-2 sp of next corner shell; rep from first * to first shell in corner. Work rem corners and sides as established; join to top of ch-3.

Rnd 4: Sl st to next ch-2 sp, work a beg shell in same sp; * trc around post of next trc, shell in ch-2 sp of next shell; rep from * to first shell of next corner; work shell in shell, trc around post of next trc, shell in shell; rep from first * to next corner. Work rem corners and sides as established; join to top of ch-3.

Rnd 5: Sl st to next ch-2 sp, work a beg shell in same sp; (trc around post of corner trc, ch 2, trc around same post as last trc, shell in ch-2 sp of next shell; * trc around post of next trc, shell in ch-2 sp of next shell; rep from * to first shell of next corner **; work shell in shell) 4 times, end last rep at **; join to top of ch-3; fasten off.

Rnd 6: (*Note:* Ch-2 sp at corners establish the corner points for the next 4 rnds.) Join yarn in ch-2 sp of any corner, work a beg shell; * trc around post of next trc, shell

continued

in ch-2 sp of next shell; rep from * to ch-2 corner sp; work shell in this sp; rep from first * to next ch-2 corner sp. Work rem corners and sides as established; join to top of beg ch-3.

Rnd 7–11: Rep rnds 2–6.

Rnds 12–16: Rep rnds 2–6.

Rnd 17: Work 1 rnd of reverse sc (work from left to right) around working sc in each st and each ch-sp; work 3 sc in each corner; fasten off.

Weave ribbons through beading sts in center rectangle. Tack ribbons in place to secure.

Embroidered Jacket And Cap

Shown on page 42.

Directions are for infant size 6 months. Changes for sizes 12 and 18 months follow in parentheses. The finished crocheted chest measurements are 20 (21½, 23) inches.

MATERIALS

Coats & Clark Red Heart Sofspun baby yarn (2-ounce skein): 2 (2, 3) skeins of white

Size E aluminum crochet hook or size to obtain gauge

J. & P. Coats Deluxe six-strand floss: 2 skeins each rose (No. 46) and blue (No. 69)

3 yards of ⅜-inch-wide white satin ribbon

Yarn needle for embroidery

Abbreviations: See page 78.

Gauge: (V st, shell) 2 times = 2½ inches.

INSTRUCTIONS

PATTERN STITCH: *Row 1:* Ch 3 for first dc, sk next st, * **in next st work 2 dc, ch 1, and 2 dc—shell made;** sk 2 sts, **in next st work dc, ch 1, and dc—V st made;** sk 2 sts; rep from * across; end with shell, sk 1 st, dc in last st; ch 3, turn.

Row 2: * Shell in ch-1 sp of shell, V st in ch-1 sp of V st; rep from * across; end shell in last shell, dc in third ch of starting ch; ch 3, turn.

Rep Row 2 for pat st.

For the jacket

BACK: Beg at bottom, with white, ch 66 (72, 78).

Foundation row: Sc in second ch from hook and in each ch across—65 (71, 77) sc. Turn.

Row 1: Work Row 1 of pat st—11 (12, 13) shells across.

Row 2: Rep Row 2 of pat st; ch 3, turn.

Row 3 (dec row): In ch-1 sp of shell work dc, ch 1, and 2 dc, work in pat st across; in last ch-1 shell sp work 2 dc, ch 1, and dc; dc in top of turning-ch; ch 4 for first dc and for ch-1 on next row, turn.

Row 4 (dec row): 2 dc in ch-1 sp of shell; work in pat st to last shell; in last ch-1 shell sp work 2 dc and ch 1; dc in top of turning-ch; ch 3, turn.

Row 5 (dec row): 2 dc in ch-1 sp, work in pat st across; end 2 dc in turning lp, dc in third ch of turning ch-4; ch 3, turn.

Row 6 (dec row): Dc in next 2 dc; work in pat st across; end dc in last 2 dc, dc in top of turning-ch; ch 3, turn.

Row 7 (dec row): V st in ch-1 sp of V st; work in pat st across; end V st in ch-1 sp of last V st, dc in top of turning-ch—rows 3–7 dec 1 shell at each side.

Rows 8–16 (17, 18): Work even in pat st across, beg and ending each row with a V st. Do not ch 3 to turn at end of last row.

ARMHOLE SHAPING: Sl st to second dc of first shell, ch 3, dc in ch-1 sp of shell; work in pat st across; end dc in ch-1 sp of last shell, dc in next dc; ch 3, turn. (Leave last V st unworked.)

Next row: V st in ch-1 sp of V st; work in pat st across; end V st in last V st, dc in top of turning-ch; ch 3, turn.

Work even in pat st until 9 (10, 11) rows above armhole shaping; do not ch 3 at end of last row.

SHOULDER AND NECK SHAPING: Sl st over V st and next shell; work V st in next V st, shell in shell, V st in V st; fasten off. Work opposite side to correspond.

RIGHT FRONT: With white, ch 36 (42, 48).

Foundation row: Sc in second ch from hook and in each ch across—35 (41, 47) sc; ch 3, turn.

Row 1: Work Row 1 of pat st across; ch 3, turn.

Row 2: Rep Row 2 of pat st; ch 3, turn.

Rows 3–7: Cont to work in pat st, and, at same time, work dec shell on *one* side following dec directions for Back (rows 3–7). Work until same length as back to armhole; end at arm edge or same side as dec edge.

ARMHOLE SHAPING AND YOKE: Sl st to center of next shell, work 23 (27, 31) sc evenly spaced across front edge; ch 1, turn.

Next row (sc-dec row): Sc in 21 (25, 29) sc; **draw up lp in each of next 2 sc, yo, and draw through 3 lps on hook—sc-dec made**—22 (26, 30) sc; ch 1, turn.

Next row: Work even in sc; ch 1, turn.

Next row: Rep sc-dec row—21 (25, 29) sc; ch 1, turn.

Cont in sc, work even until piece measures 1 inch less than back to shoulder shaping, end at arm edge; ch 1, turn.

NECK SHAPING: Sc to last 6 (7,8) sc, leave rem sts unworked for neck edge—15 (18, 21) sc.

Next row: Dec 1 sc at neck edge, complete row in sc—14 (17, 20) sc; ch 1, turn. Work until same length as back to shoulder shaping, end at neck edge.

SHOULDER SHAPING: Sc in 9 (10, 11) sc; turn.

Next row: Sl st in 2 (3, 4) sc, sc in 7 sc; fasten off.

LEFT FRONT: Work same as Right Front, reversing shaping.

SLEEVES: With white, ch 30 (36, 42).

Foundation row: Sc in second ch from hook and in each ch across—29 (35, 41) sc; ch 3, turn.

Rows 1–17 (18, 19): Beg Row 1, work in pat st.

CAP SHAPING: Sl st across shell and to center of next V st;

work row in pat st, leave last shell unworked.

Next row: Work even in pat st as established.

Eliminating 1 st per row, dec 1 V st over next 3 rows. Work even in pat st until 8 (9, 10) rows above armhole shaping; fasten off.

FINISHING: Sew shoulder seams. Sew sleeves in place, easing as necessary to fit. Sew underarm and side seams.

FRONT BORDER: *Row 1:* With right side facing, join white at bottom of front edge, sc an odd number of sts evenly spaced to neck, 3 sc in corner, sc an odd number of sts around neck, 3 sc in corner, sc an odd number of sts down rem front edge; ch 1, turn.

Row 2: Sc in first sc, * ch 2, sk sc, sc in next sc; rep from * across; fasten off.

SLEEVE BORDER: *Rnd 1:* With right side facing, join white at seam, sc an even number of sts evenly spaced around sleeve; join with sl st to first sc.

Rnd 2: Sc in first sc, * ch 2, sk sc, sc in next sc; rep from * around; join to first sc; fasten off.

EMBROIDERY: Use four strands of floss for straight stitches; use two strands for French knots. Sk first row of sc on bottom of yoke. Refer to chart, *right,* to work stitches and floss colors.

RIBBON TIES: For front, cut two 10-inch lengths. Tie through ch-2 loops at neck and bottom of yoke. For sleeves, cut two 10-inch lengths. Draw through several sts about 3 rows up from bottom of sleeve. Tie in bows.

For the cap

CAP BACK: Ch 18 (18, 24).

Foundation row: Sc in second ch from hook and in each ch across—17 (17, 23) sc; ch 3, turn.

Row 1: Sk next sc, * V st in next st, sk 2 sc, shell in next st, sk 2 sc; rep from * across; cnd with V st, sk 1 st, dc in last st; ch 3, turn—2 (2, 3) shells.

Rows 2–10 (11, 12): Cont in pat st as established, with a V st at each edge. At end of last row, fasten off.

TOP AND SIDES: Ch 66 (66, 72).

Foundation row: Sc in second ch from hook and in each ch across—65 (65, 71) sc; ch 3, turn.

Row 1: Rep Row 1 of Cap Back—10 (10, 11) shells.

Rows 2–8 (8, 9): Cont in pat st as established, with a V st at each edge. At end of last row, ch 1, turn.

Next row: Work 60 (66, 70) sc evenly across; ch 1, turn.

JACKET

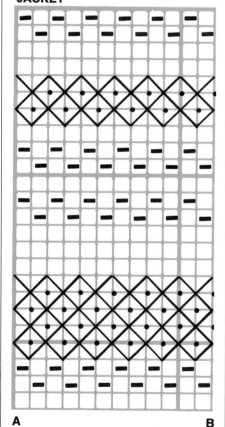

A   B

CAP

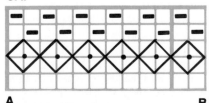

A   B

⊟ **Straight stitch with blue**
◇ **Straight stitches with rose**
⊡ **French knot with blue**

Next 7 (8, 9) rows: Sc in each sc across; ch 1, turn.

Last row: Sc in first sc, * ch 2, sk 2 sc, sc in next sc; rep from * across; fasten off.

FINISHING: Arrange beg ch of top and sides around three sides of back (on back, beg ch edge is free edge). Sew the two pieces tog, easing as necessary to fit. With right side facing, join white at bottom corner; sc evenly across side, across bottom of back, then across rem side; fasten off.

EMBROIDERY: Begin embroidery 1 sc row above last pat-st row. Referring to chart, *left,* work embroidery stitches on cap in sc border stitches. For ties, cut remaining ribbon into 18-inch lengths. Tie top of each length into a bow; sew bows to edges of cap.

Double-Breasted Jacket and Cap

Shown on page 43.

Directions are for infant size 6 months. Changes for sizes 12 and 18 months follow in parentheses. Finished chest measurements are 22 (23, 24) inches.

MATERIALS
Coats & Clark Red Heart Sofspun baby yarn (2-ounce skein): 2 (3, 3) skeins robin blue (No. 814), 1 skein white.
Size E aluminum crochet hook or size to obtain gauge
Ten ½-inch-diameter buttons

Abbreviations: See page 78.
Gauge: 2 pat sts = 1 inch.

INSTRUCTIONS
PATTERN STITCH: *Row 1:* In second ch from hook work sc, ch 1, and hdc; sk 2 ch, * in next ch work sc, ch 1, and hdc; sk 2 ch; rep from * across; end sc in last ch; ch 2, turn.

continued

Row 2: **In next hdc work sc, ch 1, and hdc—1 pat-grp made;** rep from * across; end hdc in last sc; ch 1, turn.

Row 3: Sc in first hdc; * work pat-grp in next hdc; rep from * across; end sc in top of turning ch-2; ch 2, turn. Rep rows 2 and 3 for pat st.

For the jacket

BACK: With blue yarn, ch 65 (68, 71). Work in pat st until 6½ (7, 7½) inches from beg, or the desired length to underarm—21 (22, 23) pat-grp. Place marker at each edge for underarm. Cont in pat st as established until 4½ (4¾, 5¼) inches above markers.

NECK SHAPING: Work in pat st until 8 (8, 9) pat-grp are completed, sc in next hdc; fasten off. Work other shoulder to correspond, reversing shaping.

LEFT FRONT: With blue yarn, ch 35 (38, 41). Work in pat st same as Back until 2 inches above armhole markers—11 (12, 13) pat-grp; end at armhole edge.

V-NECK SHAPING: *Row 1:* Work in pat st across 10 (11, 12) pat-grp, **sc in hdc of next grp—1 pat-grp-dec at neck edge made;** ch 2, turn.

Row 2: Work in pat st.

Rep rows 1 and 2 until 8 (8, 9) pat-grp rem. Work until same length as back. Fasten off.

RIGHT FRONT: Work same as Left Front, reversing shaping.

FIRST SLEEVE: With blue, ch 53 (56, 59).

Rows 1–2: Work in pat st on 17 (18, 19) pat-grp. Do not ch 1 at end of Row 2.

Row 3 (dec row): **Sl st to hdc of first pat-grp—dec at beg of row;** ch 1, work in pat st across, end **sc in hdc of last pat-grp—dec at end of row—**15 (16, 17) pat-grp; ch 2, turn.

Row 4: Work even in pat st.

Row 5: Rep Row 3—13 (14, 15) pat-grp.

Work even and cont in pat st as established until 8½ (8¾, 9) inches from beg.

Next row: Sc evenly across; fasten off blue.

Next row: Join white in first st, ch 1, sc in each st; fasten off.

SECOND SLEEVE: Work same as First Sleeve, except work rows 1–4 with white; fasten off white. Join blue on Row 5 to complete sleeve.

FINISHING: Sew the shoulder seams. Sew sleeves in place from marker to marker: blue sleeve on right side, blue and white sleeve on left side. Sew underarm and side seams.

FRONT BORDER: *Rnd 1:* With right side facing, join blue at side seam, ch 1; sc evenly to front corner, work 3 sc in corner; sc evenly up one of front openings, around V-neck, and down opposite front opening; 3 sc at bottom corner, sc across remainder of bottom. Join to first sc; fasten off blue.

Rnd 2: On left side, mark for 5 button lps. Position one lp ½ inch from bottom and one lp ½ inch from V-neck; position the rem 3 lps evenly spaced between the top and bottom markings. Join white, work around in sc; work 3 sc at each corner as before. Opposite each marker, work button lp as follows: Sc in st before marker, ch 2, sk sc, sc in next st. At end of rnd, join to first sc. Fasten off.

Overlap front 1½ (1½, 2) inches. Sew buttons in place opposite button lps. Sew another 5 buttons in place on the button-lp side 1½ (1½, 2) inches to right of lps.

For the cap

CAP: With blue, ch 68.

Row 1: Sc in second ch from hook and in each ch across—67 sc; ch 1, turn.

Row 2: Working in back lps, sc in each sc across; ch 1, turn.

Rows 3–48 (50, 52): Rep Row 2.

Next row: In first sc work sc, ch 1, and hdc, sk 2 sc; * in next sc work sc, ch 1, and hdc, sk 2 sc; rep from * across; end sc in last sc; ch 1, turn.

Next 9 rows: Beg with Row 3, cont in pat st same as jacket. At end of last row, fasten off blue.

Next 4 (5, 6) rows: With white,

cont in pat st. At end of last row, fasten off white.

Next 10 rows: Join blue, cont in pat st. Fasten off.

FINISHING: Sew the last row of pat st to starting ch. With a yarn needle, sew around top of cap with short gathering stitches. Draw top together; secure yarn end. To make the pom-pom, wind white yarn around a 2-inch-wide strip of cardboard 100 times. Remove the yarn from the cardboard strip and tie a double strand of yarn around the center of the bundle. Trim the loops; sew pom-pom to top of cap.

Mama and Baby Polar-Bear Toys

Shown on pages 44–45.

Mama bear is 12 inches tall; baby bear is 9 inches tall.

MATERIALS

For mama bear

Coats & Clark Red Heart 4-ply knit and crochet yarn (3½-ounce skein): 1 skein of white

Size F aluminum crochet hook or size to obtain gauge

For baby bear

Coats & Clark Red Heart Sofspun Pompadour 3-ply yarn, (3-ounce skein): 1 skein of white (also used for trim on both bear outfits)

Size E aluminum crochet hook or size to obtain gauge

For both bears

Coats & Clark Red Heart Sofspun 3-ply baby yarn, (3-ounce skein): 1 skein pink (No. 722) for bear outfits

Tapestry needle for smocking

2 yards of gray 4-ply yarn for embroidery

Polyester fiberfill

Abbreviations: See page 78.

Gauge: With Size F hook and 4-ply yarn: 9 sc = 2 inches; 9 rnds = 2 inches. With Size E hook and 3-ply yarn: 11 sc = 2 inches; 11 rnds = 2 inches.

INSTRUCTIONS
For mama bear

HEAD AND BODY: Beg at top of head with Size F hook and white 4-ply yarn, ch 2.

Rnd 1: Work 6 sc in second ch from hook. Do not join rnds; carry a contrasting color yarn up between last and first sc to indicate beg of each rnd.

Rnd 2: Work 2 sc in each sc around—12 sc.

Rnd 3: (Sc in next sc; **2 sc in next sc—inc made**) 6 times—18 sc.

Rnd 4: (Sc in next 2 sc, inc in next sc) 6 times—24 sc.

Rnd 5: Sc in each sc around.

Rnd 6: (Sc in next 3 sc, inc in next sc) 6 times—30 sc.

Rnd 7: (Sc in next 4 sc, inc in next sc) 6 times—36 sc.

Rnds 8-12: Rep Rnd 5.

Rnd 13: Inc in each of next 6 sc—cheek started; sc in next 6 sc; inc in each of next 6 sc—other cheek started; sc in next 18 sc —48 sc.

Rnds 14-16: Rep Rnd 5.

Rnd 17: (**Draw up lp in each of next 2 sc, yo, and draw through all 3 lps on hook—dec made**) 6 times; sc in next 6 sc, (dec over next 2 sc) 6 times; sc in next 18 sc—36 sc.

Rnd 18: (Sc in next 4 sc, dec over next 2 sc) 6 times.

Rnd 19: (Sc in next 3 sc, dec over next 2 sc) 6 times.

Rnd 20: (Sc in next 2 sc, dec over next 2 sc) 6 times—18 sc.

Stuff head. Place markers on sides of head on rnds 5 and 10 for placement of ears.

Rnds 21-23: Rep Rnd 5.

Rnd 24: (Sc in next 2 sc, inc in next sc) 6 times.

Rnd 25: (Sc in next 3 sc, inc in next sc) 6 times.

Rnd 26: (Sc in next 4 sc, inc in next sc) 6 times.

Rnd 27: (Sc in next 5 sc, inc in next sc) 6 times—42 sc.

Rnd 28-42: Rep Rnd 5.

Rnd 43: (Sc in next 5 sc, dec over next 2 sc) 6 times.

Rnds 44-46: Rep rnds 18-20. Stuff body.

Rnd 47: (Sc in next sc, dec over next 2 sc) 6 times—12 sc.

Rnd 48: (Dec over next 2 sc) 6 times; fasten off, leaving a 10-inch end. Draw end through sts of last rnd; pull together and secure with knot.

MUZZLE: Beg at center, ch 2.

Rnd 1: Work 6 sc in second ch from hook. Do not join rnds; carry yarn as before.

Rnd 2: Sc in each sc around.

Rnd 3: Inc in each sc around—12 sc.

Rnd 4: Rep Rnd 2.

Rnd 5: (Sc in next sc, inc in next sc) 6 times—18 sc.

Rnd 6: Rep Rnd 2; fasten off, leaving an end for sewing. Place a small amount of stuffing behind the muzzle and sew between cheeks on front of head.

EAR (make 2): Ears are circular forms that are crocheted, then flattened to double thickness for sturdiness.

Beg at top, ch 2.

Rnds 1-3: Rep rnds 1-3 of Head and Body—18 sc.

Rnds 4-6: Sc in each sc around.

Rnd 7: (Dec over next 2 sc) 9 times; fasten off, leaving a 10-inch end for sewing. To shape each ear, flatten piece and sew sts of last rnd together to form a flat edge; sew this edge to side of head between markers.

ARM (make 2): Starting at paw, ch 2.

Rnds 1-2: Rep rnds 1 and 2 of Head and Body—12 sc. Do not join rnds; carry yarn as before for markers.

Rnd 3: Sc in each sc around.

Rnd 4: (Sc in next 2 sc, inc in next sc) 4 times—16 sc.

Rnds 5-18: Rep Rnd 3. Stuff arm.

Rnd 19: (Dec over next 2 sc) 8 times; fasten off, leaving a 10-inch end. Draw end through sts of last rnd; pull together and secure. Sew arms in place.

LEG (make 2): Beg at top, ch 2.

Rnds 1-3: Rep rnds 1-3 of Head and Body.

Rnd 4: (Sc in next 8 sc, inc in next sc) 2 times—20 sc.

Rnds 5-13: Sc in each sc around.

Rnd 14: Inc in each of next 4 sc—shaping for top of foot started; sc in next 16 sc.

Rnds 15-17: Sc in each sc around. Stuff leg.

Rnd 18: (Sc in next 2 sc, dec over next 2 sc) 6 times.

Rnd 19: (Sc in next sc, dec over next 2 sc) 6 times.

Rnd 10: (Dec over next 2 sc) 6 times; fasten off, leaving a 10-inch end; close opening as before. Sew legs in place.

With tapestry needle and gray yarn, embroider nose, mouth, and eyes using straight stitches as shown in photo on page 44.

DRESS FRONT: Front of dress is worked vertically from top to bottom. With pink and Size E hook, ch 30.

Row 1: Sc in second ch from hook and in next 12 ch for bodice; hdc in next 16 ch for skirt; ch 2, turn.

Row 2 (right side): Hdc in first 16 hdc, sc in back lp of next 13 sc; ch 1, turn.

Row 3: Sc in back lp of first 13 sc; hdc in both lps of next 16 hdc; do not work in top of ch-2; ch 2, turn.

Rows 4-22: Rep rows 2 and 3 alternately; end with Row 2; fasten off.

DRESS BACK (make two): Work same as rows 1-11 of Dress Front; fasten off.

SMOCKING: Smocking is worked on front of dress using the vertical ridges created by sc rows. With white Pompadour yarn and tapestry needle, and with right side facing, catch two adjacent sc ridges and draw together with a straight stitch; work in this manner across. Picking up alternate ridges, work smocking on every other row.

Sew back sections to front section along shoulders. Sew side seams starting at bottom; sew seam to last hdc (sc sts are left free for armhole opening).

continued

ARMHOLE RUFFLES: With right side facing and Size E hook, join white Pompadour yarn at underarm with sl st.

Rnd 1: Ch 2, work 3 hdc in each st around armhole; join to top of ch-2; fasten off.

Rnd 2: Join pink at underarm, ch 1, sc in joining and in each hdc around; join to first sc; fasten off.

Rep ruffle edging around opposite underarm.

BODICE TRIM AND SKIRT RUFFLE: With right side facing and Size E hook, join white Pompadour yarn to first sc at waist on left side of back opening.

Rnd 1: Ch 1, sc in each sc to neck edge, make 3 sc in corner at neck edge, sc across neck edge, make 3 sc in corner at neck edge, sc in each sc along other side of back opening to waist, make 3 hdc in each of next 16 hdc, make 3 hdc in each st across bottom, 3 hdc in each of last 16 hdc; join to first sc; fasten off.

Rnd 2: Join pink in any st, ch 1, sc in joining and in each st around; join to first sc; fasten off.

Place dress on bear and sew the back edges tog from neck to bodice waist.

PANTIES (make 2): With pink and Size E hook, ch 22.

Row 1: Hdc in third ch from hook and in each ch across; ch 2, turn—20 hdc.

Rows 2–5: Hdc in each hdc across, do not work in top of ch-2; ch 2, turn. At end of Row 5, ch 1, turn.

Row 6: Sl st in first 7 hdc, ch 2, hdc in next 6 hdc; do not work over rem sts; ch 2, turn.

Rows 7–9: Hdc in each hdc; ch 2, turn. At end of Row 9, fasten off.

Sew sections together along sides; sew crotch seam.

LEG RUFFLES: Join pink at crotch seam.

Rnd 1: Ch 1, work 30 sc around leg opening; join to first sc. Do not fasten off pink.

Rnd 2: Join white Pompadour yarn, ch 2, work 3 hdc in each st around leg opening; join to top of ch-2; fasten off.

Rnd 3: With pink, ch 1, sc in joining and in each hdc around; join to first sc; fasten off.

Rep ruffle edging on opposite leg opening.

For baby bear

With Size E hook and white Pompadour yarn, work same as Mama Bear.

PLAYSUIT BACK: Starting at crotch with pink and Size E hook, ch 6.

Row 1: Hdc in third ch from hook, hdc in next 3 ch; ch 2, turn.

Rows 2–4: Sk first hdc, hdc in next 3 hdc, hdc in top of ch-2; ch 2, turn. At end of last row, ch 8, turn.

Row 5: Hdc in third ch from hook and in next 5 ch, hdc in next 4 hdc, hdc in top of ch-2, ch 7, fasten off; do not turn.

Join yarn to top of last hdc made, hdc in each of next 7 ch—19 hdc, counting ch-2 as 1 hdc. Ch 2, turn.

Row 6: Hdc in next hdc and in each hdc across to ch-2, hdc in top of ch-2; ch 2, turn.

Rep Row 6 until side measures 1½ inches. Do not ch 2 at end of last row.

ARMHOLE SHAPING: *Row 1:* Sl st in first 4 sts, ch 2, hdc in next 12 sts, do not work in last 3 sts—12 hdc; ch 2, turn.

Rows 2–5: Work even in hdc; ch 2, turn.

NECK SHAPING: *Row 6:* Hdc in next 2 hdc; ch 2, turn.

Rows 7–9: Work in hdc as before, fasten off.

Sk next 7 hdc on last long row worked; join yarn to next st.

Row 10: Ch 2, hdc in last 2 sts; ch 2, turn. Complete as for other side.

PLAYSUIT FRONT: *Row 1:* Working along opposite side of starting chain of Playsuit Back, join yarn to first ch, ch 2, hdc in next 4 ch; ch 2, turn.

Beg with Row 2, complete as for Playsuit Back.

Sew crotch, side, and shoulder seams.

LEG AND ARMHOLE RUFFLES: Work leg ruffles same as ruffles on Mama Bear Panties and armhole ruffles same as ruffles on her dress. Slip suit on Baby Bear.

Cardigan With Pockets

Shown on page 44.

Directions are for infant size 6 months. Changes for sizes 12 and 18 months follow in parentheses. Finished crocheted chest measurements are 20¾ (22, 23½) inches.

MATERIALS

Coats & Clark Red Heart Sofspun Pompadour yarn (3-ounce skein): 2 (3, 4) skeins of mint green (No. 677), 1 skein of white
Size E aluminum crochet hook or size to obtain gauge
Six ½-inch-diameter buttons

Abbreviations: See page 78.
Gauge: Pat st (11 sts) = 2 inches. Be sure to check your gauge before starting sweater.

INSTRUCTIONS

BACK: Beg at bottom, with green, ch 58 (62, 66).

Row 1: Sc in second ch from hook; * dc in next ch, sc in next ch; rep from * across; ch 3, turn—57 (61, 65) sts.

Row 2: * Sc in dc, dc in sc; rep from * across; ch 1, turn.

Row 3: * Sc in dc, dc in sc; rep from * across; end sc in top of turning ch-3; ch 3, turn.

Rep rows 2–3 for pat st. *Note:* When row ends with a sc in the last st, ch 3 to turn, counting ch 3 as first dc of next row; then sc in *next* dc to begin the row. When row ends with a dc in the last st, ch 1 to turn and sc in the *first* dc to begin the row.

Cont to work in pat st as established until 6 (6, 7) inches from beg; end with Row 2 of pat st.

ARMHOLE SHAPING: Sl st over 4 sts, rep Row 3 of pat st to last 4 sts; leave rem sts of row unworked—49 (53, 57) sts.

Next 4 rows: Dec 1 st at beg of next 4 rows as follows: **draw up lp in each of next 2 sts, yo, draw through 3 lps on hook—sc-dec made**; cont in pat st across row—45 (49, 53) sts at end of fourth row.

Keeping to pat, work even until 4 (4½, 5) inches above beg of armhole shaping.

SHOULDER AND NECK SHAPING: Sl st over 4 (6, 8) sts; work in pat across 11 sts; leave remainder of row unworked; turn.

Next row: Work in pat across 6 sts; fasten off.

Next row: Sk center 15 sts; join yarn in next st; complete rem side to correspond, reversing shaping; fasten off.

RIGHT FRONT: Beg at bottom, with green, ch 26 (28, 30).

Row 1: Rep Row 1 of Back—25 (27, 29) sts.

Cont in pat as established until same length as back to underarm, end with Row 2 of pat st.

Next row (armhole edge): Sl st across 4 sts, rep Row 3 of pat st across row; ch 3, turn—21 (23, 25) sts.

Next row: Work across in pat to last 2 sts; dec over last 2 sts; turn.

Next row: Work dec over first 2 sts; work in pat across row—19 (21, 23) sts.

Cont in pat with no dec until work measures 1 inch less than back to beg of shoulder shaping, end at neck edge.

NECK SHAPING: Sl st across 5 sts, complete row in pat.

Next row: Work across in pat to last 5 sts, leave rem sts unworked; turn.

Next row: Sl st across 5 sts, complete row in pat.

Work until front measures the same length as the back to shoulder edge, end at armhole edge—9 (11, 13) sts.

SHOULDER SHAPING: Sl st over 4 (4, 4) sts; work in pat st over 5 (7, 9) sts; turn.

Next row: Work in pat across rem sts; fasten off.

LEFT FRONT: Work same as Back, reversing shaping.

SLEEVES: Beg at bottom, with green, ch 34 (38-42).

Row 1: Sc in second ch from hook, * dc in next ch, sc in next ch; rep from * across; ch 3, turn—33 (37, 41) sts.

Rows 2-5: Work in pat as established for Back.

Row 6 (inc row): In first st work dc—inc; continue across row in pat st; in last st work 2 dc; ch 3, turn—35 (39, 43) sts.

Cont in pat, and, at same time, inc 1 st at each edge every fourth row 2 times more—39 (43, 47) sts. Work even in pat st until 5½ (6, 6½) inches from beg.

SHAPE CAP: Sl st over 4 sts, work across in pat st to last 4 sts, leave last 4 sts unworked—31 (35, 39) sts; turn.

Dec 1 st at *each edge* on next 4 rows—23 (27, 31) sts. Dec 1 st at *end* of each row until 12 (12, 14) sts rem; fasten off.

Sew shoulder seams.

With right side of sleeve facing and piece turned so you can work across the cap, join yarn at underarm and sc evenly to opposite side of underarm; fasten off. Rep on other sleeve.

With right side of armhole facing, join yarn at underarm and sc evenly around armhole opening; fasten off. Rep on other armhole.

Working through back lps of sc borders, sew sleeves to armholes. Sew underarm and side seams.

POCKET (make 2): With green, ch 12 (14, 14).

Row 1: Sc in second ch from hook, * dc in next ch, sc in next ch; rep from * across—11 (13, 13) sc.

Continue in pat st for 9 (11, 11) rows; fasten off.

WAIST RIBBING: With white, ch 10 (12, 12).

Row 1: Sc in second ch from hook and in each ch across; ch 1, turn—9 (11, 11) sc.

Row 2: Working in back lps only, sc in each sc across; ch 1, turn.

Rep Row 2 until piece, lightly stretched, fits around bottom of sweater; fasten off. Sew ribbing to sweater.

NECK RIBBING: With white, ch 7. Rep rows 1 and 2 of Waist Ribbing over 6 sc until piece, slightly stretched, fits around neck edge; fasten off. Sew ribbing around neck.

CUFF RIBBING (make 2): With white, ch 9. Rep rows 1 and 2 of Waist Ribbing over 8 sc until piece fits around edge of sleeve; fasten off. Sew ribbing to cuff; sew short edges together.

POCKET RIBBING: With white, ch 5 (7, 7). Rep rows 1 and 2 of Waist Ribbing over 4 (6, 6) sc until piece fits across top of pocket; fasten off. Sew ribbing in place. Sew pockets to front of sweater 1½ inches from side seams and at top of waist ribbing.

FRONT RIBBING (button band: left side for girl, right side for boy): With white, ch 9. Rep rows 1 and 2 of Waist Ribbing over 8 sc until piece, unstretched, fits front edge, including waist and neck ribbings. Sew band in place. Mark for six buttons, the first mark ½ inch from bottom and the sixth mark ½ inch from neck edge. Evenly space the rem four button marks between.

FRONT RIBBING (buttonhole band): With white, ch 9. Work in ribbing same as button-band ribbing to first marker.

Buttonhole row: Sc in 3 sc, ch 1, sk sc, sc in 4 sc; ch 1, turn.

Next row: Sc across in ribbing, working sc in ch-1 sp. Cont working in ribbing to next marker; work Buttonhole Row. When band is completed; fasten off. Sew band on rem front edge. Sew buttons in place.

Irish-Rose Blanket And Pillow

Shown on pages 46 and 47.

Blanket is 36x47 inches. Pillow is 12 inches square.

MATERIALS
For the blanket
DMC Cotonia (50-gram ball): 12 balls of white
Size 1 steel crochet hook
Blunt-end tapestry needle
Safety pin

For the pillow
DMC Cotonia (50-gram ball): 2 balls of white
Size 1 steel crochet hook
Blunt-end tapestry needle
12-inch-square satin pillow

Abbreviations: See page 78.
Gauge: One rose motif is 3½ inches square.

INSTRUCTIONS
FIRST ROSE MOTIF: Ch 5, join with sl st to form ring.
Rnd 1: Ch 1, work 12 sc in ring; join with sl st to front lp of first sc.
Rnd 2: * Ch 3, sl st in front lp of next sc; rep from * 11 times more.
Rnd 3: Sl st into back lp of same sc; * ch 3, sk next sc, sl st in back lp of next sc; repeat from * 4 times more; end ch 3, sl st in first ch-lp of rnd—6 ch-3 lps.
Rnd 4: Ch 1, in *each* ch-3 lp of Rnd 3 work **sc, 3 dc, and sc— small petal made;** join with sl st to first ch-1 sp of rnd—6 petals.
Rnd 5: (Ch 4, sl st in back lp of first sc of next petal) 5 times; ch 4, sl st in first ch-4 lp—6 ch-4 lps.
Rnd 6: Ch 1, in *each* ch-4 lp around work **sc, 5 dc, and sc— large petal made.** Join with sl st in ch-1 sp—6 petals.
Rnd 7: Sl st to first dc; ch 1, sc in same st as sl st; (ch 5, sk 3 dc, sc in next dc; ch 5, sc in first dc of next petal) 6 times; join last ch-5 with sl st to first sc at beg of rnd.
Rnd 8: Sl st in next 3 ch, ch 1, sc in lp; * ch 5, sc in next lp; rep from * around; end ch 5, join with sl st to first sc—12 ch-5 lps.

Rnd 9: Sl st in next 3 ch, ch 1, sc in lp; * ch 5, sc in next lp (mark this st with safety pin), ch 1, turn; work 7 sc in ch-5 lp just made; ch 1, turn; sc in 7 sc, sl st in sc marked with safety pin. (Ch 5, sc in next lp) 2 times; rep from * 3 times more; join with sl st at base of 7-sc grp.
Rnd 10: Sl st in first sc at top of 7-sc grp; ch 1, sc in same st; * (ch 5, sk 2 sc, sc in next sc) 2 times; (ch 5, sc in next ch-5 lp) 2 times; ch 5, sc in first sc of 7-sc grp; rep from * 3 times more; join last ch-5 to first sc of rnd. Fasten off.

SECOND ROSE MOTIF: Work same as First Rose Motif through Rnd 9.
Rnd 10 (joining rnd): Sl st in first sc at top of 7-sc grp, ch 1, sc in same st; ch 5, sk 2 sc, sc in next sc, ch 2; with wrong sides of two motifs facing, sl st in matching ch-5 lp on top of 7-sc grp of first motif; ch 2, sk 2 sc on motif in progress, sc in next sc, (ch 2, sl st in next lp on first motif, ch 2, sc in next lp of motif in progress) 2 times; ch 2, sl st in next lp of first motif, ch 2, sc in first sc of 7-sc grp of motif in progress; ch 2, sl st in next lp of first motif, ch 2, sk 2 sc on motif in progress, sc in next sc; * ch 5, sk 2 sc, sc in next sc; (ch 5, sc in next lp) 2 times; ch 5, sc in first sc of grp; ch 5, sk 2 sc, sc in next sc; rep from * 1 time more; ch 5, sk 2 sc, sc in next sc; (ch 5, sc in next lp) 2 times; ch 5, join with sl st to first sc; fasten off.

TRIANGLE MOTIF: Ch 30.
Row 1: Sc in front lp of second ch from hook and in front lp of each ch across row, ch 1, turn— 29 sc.
Row 2: **Draw up lp in front lp of first sc, draw up lp in back lp of second sc, yo, draw through 3 lps on hook—sc-dec made.** * Sc in front lp of next sc, sc in back lp of next sc; rep from * across until 2 sc remain. Work sc-dec over last 2 sc, ch 1, turn.
Rows 3–13: Rep Row 2—5 sts rem at end of Row 13.
Row 14: Work even; fasten off.

SHAPED SQUARE: Ch 6.
Row 1: Sc in front lp of second ch from hook and in each ch across row, ch 1, turn—5 sc.
Row 2: Sc in front lp of first sc, (sc in back lp of next sc, sc in front lp of next sc) 2 times; ch 1, turn.
Row 3: **Sc in back lp of first sc, sc in front lp of same sc—inc at beg of odd-numbered row made;** * sc in back lp of next sc, sc in front lp of next sc; rep from * across until 1 sc rem; **sc in front lp of last sc, sc in back lp of same sc—inc at end of odd-numbered row made;** ch 1, turn.
Row 4: **Sc in front lp of first sc, sc in back lp of same sc—inc at beg of even-numbered row made;** * sc in front lp of next sc, sc in back lp of next sc; rep from * across until 1 sc rem; **sc in back lp of last sc, sc in front lp of same sc—inc at end of even-numbered row made;** ch 1, turn.
Rows 5–15: Rep rows 3 and 4 alternately—31 sts at end of Row 15. Ch 4, turn at end of Row 15.
Rows 16–17: Sc in second ch from hook and in next 2 ch; work in established pat across row; ch 4, turn—37 sc at end of Row 17.
Rows 18–19: Work even in established pat.
Rows 20–21: Sl st in 4 sc, ch 1, work in pat across row; ch 1, turn.
Rows 22–34: **Draw up lp in front lp of first sc, draw up lp in back lp of second sc, yo, draw through 3 lps on hook—sc-dec made.** Continue in pat across row until 2 sts rem; sc-dec over last 2 sts; ch 1, turn—5 sts rem at end of Row 34.
Row 35: Work even; fasten off.

For the pillow
Make five Rose Motifs and join as shown in diagram, *opposite.* Make four Triangle Motifs and sew motifs in place.

CORNERS: * Attach thread in corner lp of any rose motif; (ch 5, sc in next lp) 4 times; turn; sl st to center of lp just made; (ch 5, sc in next lp) 3 times; turn; sl st to center of lp just made; ch 5, sc in next lp; fasten off. Rep from * on rem three corners.

BORDER: *Rnd 1:* Join thread in any corner lp, ch 3, in same lp work dc, ch 1, sc, 2 dc, ch 1, and sc. * In *each* of next 4 lps work **2 dc, ch 1, and sc—shell made;** shell in first st of triangle, (sk 4 sts, shell in next st) 6 times; shell in last st; shell in each of next 4 lps; 2 shells in corner lp; rep from * around; join with sl st to top of beg ch-3; turn.

Rnd 2: Sl st into ch-1 sp; ch 3, in same sp work dc, ch 1, and sc; work shell in each ch-1 sp around; join with sl st to beg ch-3.

Rnds 3–4: Rep Rnd 2; fasten off.

FINISHING: Weave in thread ends on back side of pillow. Press; sew pillow top to satin pillow with small hidden stitches.

For the blanket
Make 66 Rose Motifs and join as shown in diagram, *right.* Make 17 Shaped Squares and 24 Triangle Motifs; hand-sew squares and triangles to rose motifs to complete the top.

BORDER: *Rnd 1:* With right side facing, attach thread to corner lp of any corner rose motif. Working along one of the short sides, in the first st of triangle work **2 dc, ch 1, and sc—shell made;** (* sk 4 st, shell in next st; rep from * 6 times more; shell in last st; shell in sc of rose-motif lp, shell in first st of triangle) 5 times; shell in next 5 rose-motif lps, shell in first st of triangle; working down one of the long sides, rep bet ( )s 7 times; shell in each of next 5 rose-motif lps; continue in pat as established to complete rem 2 sides. Join with sl st to first dc.

Rnds 2–3: Sl st in ch-1 sp, ch 3, in same sp work dc, ch 1, and sc; shell in each ch-1 sp around; join with sl st to top of ch-3; turn.

Rnd 4: Sl st in ch-1 sp, ch 3; in same sp work dc, ch 1, sc, 2 dc, ch 1, and sc; * shell in each ch-1 sp across side until first ch-1 sp over

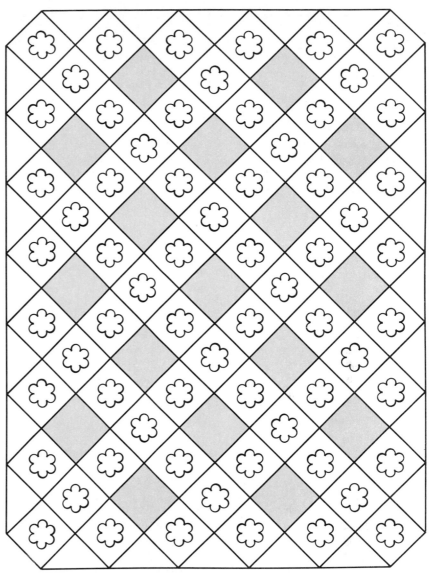

IRISH-ROSE PILLOW

Rose motif   Shaped square   Triangle motif

a rose-motif lp; in that lp work 2 shells, shell in next 3 ch-1 lps, 2 shells in next lp; rep from * to work next side and corner. Work rem 2 sides to correspond; join with sl st to top of ch-3 at beg of rnd; turn.

Rnds 5–6: Rep Rnd 2.

Rnd 7: Ch 1, sc in next sc and ch-sp; * **ch 3, sc in third ch from hook—picot made;** sk next dc, sc in dc, sc, ch-1 sp; rep from * around, ending with picot; join with sl st to first sc; fasten off.

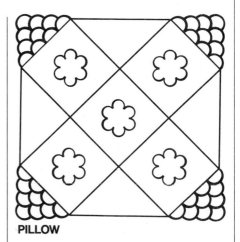

PILLOW

PRETTY AND PRACTICAL

SPREADS AND AFGHANS

Traditional designs like the ones in this chapter bring comfort, style, and individuality to your home.

The arrowhead pattern on the afghan, *below,* and the spread, *right,* is a time-honored favorite among crocheters.

Twelve 14-inch-square blocks in white and palest yellow (six of each color) make up the 44x58-inch throw. Popcorn stitches add texture to each block.

The bedspread features 12-inch-square blocks sewn together and trimmed with a border slightly more than six inches deep. Directions are given for twin-, full-, and queen-size bedspreads.

Instructions for designs in this chapter begin on page 68.

Things are not always what they seem! The six-sided medallion used in the bedspread *above,* for example, is modestly pretty to be sure, yet by itself it's unexceptional (see the closeup photo, *opposite*). But when a batch of the crocheted blocks is whipstitched together, the design develops into an expanse of swirling stars spinning dramatically across the coverlet. It's a transformation to dazzle and delight the beholder.

The bedspread measures about 84 inches square. The hexagonal motifs are about 5 inches across at the widest points.

For the full-size spread pictured, you'll need 347 motifs. (To adjust the size of the spread, stitch more or fewer medallions.)

With only eight rounds in each motif, the blocks won't take long to make. Join the motifs and trim the bedspread with a narrow shell-stitch edging.

S quares and hexagonal motifs aren't the only building blocks used in crocheted bedspreads; panels work equally well.

This filet design, for example, with its timeless geometric pattern, consists of 13-inch-wide lengths crafted individually and joined, then edged with a wide border. The spread measures 77 inches long; before the 8¼-inch-deep borders are added, the spread is 65 inches wide.

The pillow cover (see the closeup photo, *above*) is simply a single bedspread panel finished with the edging along one side.

For beds with footboards, such as this one, omit the edging at the end of the spread; stitch the edging only along the sides.

For beds without footboards, crochet sufficient border to trim the end of the spread as well as the sides.

Want some companion accessories for your bedroom? Crochet just the edging, using thread that is finer than the thread used for the spread. The edging will be narrower, and just right for trimming pillows, curtains, a tablecloth, or a dresser scarf.

SPREADS AND AFGHANS

Need a memorable gift for a college-bound teen? Treat your favorite young person to the cozy throw *opposite*. Accent it with his or her favorite colors—or school colors—woven in place after the crocheting is completed.

Or make the afghan for yourself or a friend, and embellish it with colors that complement the room in which it will eventually be at home.

Star stitches fill the areas between the woven bands on this 51x65-inch design. A lavish fringe trims the ends.

You won't have to worry about windchill and winter's other challenges when you have an afghan like this one, *above*, in the house. Just wrap yourself in its cozy warmth and forget about the weather.

Crafted of worsted yarn, with bobble stitches worked into a diamond pattern in each block, this afghan is soft, thick, and wonderful.

Crochet each of the 80 six-inch-square blocks in just six rounds. Join the blocks into 10 rows of eight blocks each for this 50x62-inch throw.

SPREADS AND AFGHANS

If you live in a warm climate, or prefer to put away your heaviest afghans when winter is past, you'll like this featherlight design. Make it in upbeat lavender and white, or other favorite colors, using lustrous cotton yarns.

The medallion design lends itself to a variety of color arrangements, including all white, as you can see in the pillows, *above* and *opposite.*

The afghan, *opposite,* measures 48x59 inches and consists of twenty 11-inch-square blocks. A graceful border of open stitches (beading)

and delicate scallops completes the afghan.

For each pillow, crochet one block. Add the edging, sew the crochet atop a chintz pillow, and thread narrow ribbon through the beading on the border. Completed pillows are about 16½ inches square.

Arrowhead-Design Bedspread

Shown on pages 58–59.

See the note *below* for bedspread sizes.

MATERIALS
Lily Sugar 'n' Cream 3-ply cotton baby and fingering yarn (1.25-ounce skein): White or color desired (3 skeins makes 2 blocks)
Size 7 steel crochet hook or size to obtain gauge
Sewing thread to match yarn

Abbreviations: See page 78.
Gauge: 7 dc = 1 inch; 3 dc rows = 1 inch; one block measures 12 inches square.

INSTRUCTIONS
Note: The spread shown is an antique and is crocheted from a coarse crochet cotton that is no longer available. The yarn listed in the materials list will produce a bedspread of similar size and texture. For a twin-size bed (60x96 inches plus border), make 40 blocks and sew them together in eight rows, each row having five blocks. For a standard-size bed (72x96 inches plus border), make 48 blocks and sew them together in eight rows, each row having six blocks. For a queen-size bed (84x108 inches plus border), make 63 blocks and sew them together in nine rows, each row having seven blocks.

For a smaller gauge block, use these instructions, Coats & Clark's Knit-Cro-Sheen mercerized bedspread cotton, and a Size 7 steel crochet hook. This thread produces a block that measures 8½ inches square and a border that measures 4½ inches wide. The amount of thread required will depend on the size of the spread you choose to make.

Ch 6, join with sl st to form ring.

Rnd 1: Ch 3, work 17 dc in ring; join with sl st in top of ch-3.

Rnd 2: Ch 3, dc in same st as join, 2 dc in *each* dc around; join with sl st to top of beg ch-3—36 dc, counting beg ch-3 as st.

Rnd 3: Ch 8, * sk next 2 dc, dc in next dc, (ch 2, sk dc, dc in next dc) 3 times, ch 5; rep from * around; end ch 2, sk dc, join with sl st to third ch of beg ch-8.

Rnd 4: Ch 3, * in corner ch-5 sp work 3 dc, ch 3, and 3 dc; dc in next dc, (ch 2, dc in next dc) 3 times; rep from * around; end dc in last dc, ch 2, join with sl st to top of ch-3 at beg of rnd.

Rnd 5: Ch 3, * dc in next 3 dc, in next corner sp work 3 dc, ch 3, and 3 dc; dc in next 4 dc, (ch 2, dc in next dc) 3 times; rep from * around; end dc in last dc, ch 2, join with sl st to top of beg ch-3.

Rnd 6: Ch 3, * dc in next 6 dc, in next corner sp work 3 dc, ch 3, and 3 dc; dc in next 7 dc, (ch 2, dc in next dc) 3 times; rep from * around; end dc in last dc, ch 2, join with sl st to top of beg ch-3.

Rnd 7: Ch 3, * dc in next 9 dc, in next corner sp work 3 dc, ch 3, and 3 dc; dc in next 10 dc, (ch 2, dc in next dc) 3 times; rep from * around; end dc in last dc, ch 2, join with sl st to top of beg ch-3.

Rnd 8: Ch 3, * dc in next 12 dc, in next corner sp work 3 dc, ch 3, and 3 dc; dc in next 13 dc, (ch 2, dc in next dc) 3 times; rep from * around; end dc in last dc, ch 2, join with sl st to top of ch-3.

Rnd 9: Ch 3, * dc in next 15 dc, in next corner sp work 3 dc, ch 3, and 3 dc; dc in next 16 dc, (ch 2, dc in next dc) 3 times; rep from * around; end dc in last dc, ch 2, join with sl st to top of ch-3.

Rnd 10: Ch 3, * dc in next 18 dc, in next corner sp work 3 dc, ch 3, and 3 dc; dc in next 19 dc, (ch 2, dc in next dc) 3 times; rep from * around; end dc in last dc, ch 2, join with sl st to top of ch-3.

Rnd 11: Ch 5, sk next 2 dc, * dc in next 19 dc; in corner st work dc, ch 3, and dc; dc in next 19 dc, ch 2, sk 2 dc, dc in next dc, (ch 2, dc in next dc) 3 times, ch 2, sk 2 dc; rep from * around; end dc in last dc, ch 2, join with sl st to third ch of beg ch-5.

Rnd 12: Ch 5, dc in next dc, ch 2, sk 2 dc, * dc in next 17 dc, ch 2, in center ch of corner sp work dc, ch 5, and dc; ch 2, dc in next 17 dc, ch 2, sk 2 dc, dc in next dc, ch 2, dc in next dc, ch 2, sk ch-2 sp, 4 dc in next sp; ch 2, sk sp, dc in next dc, ch 2, dc in next dc, ch 2, sk 2 dc; rep from * around; end 4 dc in ch-2 sp, ch 2, sk sp, join with sl st to third ch of beg ch-5.

Rnd 13: Sl st into next 2 ch and dc, ch 5, dc in next dc, ch 2, sk 2 dc, * dc in next 14 dc, ch 2, dc in next dc, ch 2, in center ch of corner sp work dc, ch 5, and dc; (ch 2, dc in next dc) 2 times; dc in next 13 dc, ch 2, sk 2 dc, dc in next dc, ch 2, dc in next dc, ch 2, sk ch-2 sp, 4 dc in next ch-2 sp, ch 2, 4 dc in next ch-2 sp, ch 2, sk sp, dc in next dc, ch 2, dc in next dc, ch 2, sk 2 dc; rep from * around; end 4 dc in ch-2 sp, ch 2, join to third ch of beg ch-5.

Rnd 14: Sl st into next 2 ch and dc, ch 5, dc in next dc, ch 2, sk 2 dc, * dc in next 11 dc, (ch 2, dc in next dc) 2 times, ch 2, in center ch of corner sp work dc, ch 5, and dc; (ch 2, dc in next dc) 3 times; dc in next 10 dc, ch 2, sk 2 dc, dc in next dc, ch 2, dc in next dc, ch 2, sk ch-2 sp, 4 dc in next ch-2 sp, (ch 2, 4 dc in next ch-2 sp) 2 times, ch 2, sk sp, dc in next dc, ch 2, dc in next dc, ch 2, sk 2 dc; rep from * around; end 4 dc in ch-2 sp, ch 2, join with sl st to third ch of beg ch-5.

Rnd 15: Sl st into next 2 ch and dc, ch 5, dc in next dc, ch 2, sk 2 dc, * dc in next 8 dc, (ch 2, dc in next dc) 3 times, ch 2, in center ch of corner sp work dc, ch 5, and dc; (ch 2, dc in next dc) 4 times; dc in next 7 dc, ch 2, sk 2 dc, dc in next dc, ch 2, dc in next dc, ch 2, sk ch-2 sp, 4 dc in next ch-2 sp, (ch 2, 4 dc in next ch-2 sp) 3 times, ch 2, sk sp, dc in next dc, ch 2, dc in next dc, ch 2, sk 2 dc; rep from * around; end 4 dc in ch-2 sp, ch 2, join to third ch of beg ch-5.

Rnd 16: Sl st into next 2 ch and dc, ch 5, dc in next dc, ch 2, sk 2 dc, * dc in next 5 dc, (ch 2, dc in next dc) 4 times, ch 2, in center ch of corner sp work dc, ch 5, and dc; (ch 2, dc in next dc) 5 times; dc in next 4 dc, ch 2, sk 2 dc, dc in next dc, ch 2, dc in next dc, ch 2, sk ch-2 sp, 4 dc in next ch-2 sp, (ch 2, 4 dc in next ch-2 sp) 4 times, ch 2, sk sp, dc in next dc, ch 2, dc in next dc, ch 2, sk 2 dc; rep from * around; end 4 dc in ch-2 sp, ch 2, join to third ch of beg ch-5.

Rnd 17: Sl st into next 2 ch and dc, ch 5, dc in next dc, ch 2, sk 2 dc, dc in next 2 dc, * (ch 2, dc in next dc) 4 times; 2 dc in ch-2 sp, dc in next dc, in ch-5 corner sp work 3 dc, ch 3, and 3 dc, dc in next dc, 2 dc in ch-2 sp, dc in next dc, (ch 2, dc in next dc) 4 times; dc in next dc, ch 2, sk 2 dc, dc in next dc, ch 2, dc in next dc, ch 2, sk ch-2 sp, 4 dc in next sp, (ch 2, 4 dc in next ch-2 sp) 5 times; ch 2, sk sp, dc in next dc, ch 2, dc in next dc, ch 2, sk 2 dc, dc in next 2 dc; rep from * around; end 4 dc in ch-2 sp, ch 2, join with sl st to third ch of beg ch-5.

Rnd 18: Sl st into next 2 ch and dc, ch 5, sk dc, dc in next dc, (ch 2, dc in next dc) 3 times; * 2 dc in ch-2 sp, dc in next 7 dc, 5 dc in ch-3 corner sp, dc in next 7 dc, 2 dc in next sp, dc in next dc, (ch 2, dc in next dc) 2 times; ch 2, sk dc, dc in next dc, ch 2, dc in next dc, ch 2, sk sp, 4 dc in next sp, (ch 2, 4 dc in next ch-2 sp) 6 times, ch 2, sk sp, dc in next dc; ch 2, sk dc, dc in next dc, (ch 2, dc in next dc) 3 times; rep from * around; end 4 dc in ch-2 sp, ch 2, join with sl st to third ch of beg ch-5. Fasten off.

ASSEMBLY: Use double strand of matching color sewing thread to sew blocks together for desired size bedspread.

BORDER: Work the border in sufficient length to fit around three or four sides of spread, allowing several extra inches for fullness at each corner. It is best not to fasten off the border strip until it is sewn to the spread.

Row 1: Ch 44, dc in fourth ch from hook; (ch 2, sk 2 ch, dc in next ch) 13 times, dc in last ch; ch 3, turn.

Row 2: Sk first dc, dc in next dc, (ch 2, dc in next dc) 5 times; ch 2, sk sp, 4 dc in next sp, ch 2, sk sp, dc in next dc, (ch 2, dc in next dc) 5 times; dc in top of turning ch; ch 3, turn.

Row 3: Sk first dc, dc in next dc, (ch 2, dc in next dc) 4 times, ch 2, sk next sp, 4 dc in next sp, ch 2, 4 dc in next sp; ch 2, sk next sp, dc in next dc, (ch 2, dc in next dc) 4 times; dc in top of turning ch; ch 3, turn.

Row 4: Sk first dc, dc in next dc, (ch 2, dc in next dc) 3 times, ch 2, sk next sp, 4 dc in next sp, (ch 2, 4 dc in next sp) 2 times; ch 2, sk next sp, dc in next dc, (ch 2, dc in next dc) 3 times; dc in top of turning ch; ch 3, turn.

Row 5: Sk first dc, dc in next dc, (ch 2, dc in next dc) 2 times, ch 2, sk next sp, 4 dc in next sp, (ch 2, 4 dc in next sp) 3 times; ch 2, sk next sp, dc in next dc, (ch 2, dc in next dc) 2 times; dc in top of turning ch; ch 3, turn.

Row 6: Sk first dc, dc in next dc, ch 2, dc in next dc, ch 2, sk next sp, 4 dc in next sp, (ch 2, 4 dc in next sp) 4 times; ch 2, sk next sp, dc in next dc, ch 2, dc in next dc; dc in top of turning ch; ch 3, turn.

Row 7: Sk first dc, dc in next dc, (ch 2, dc in next dc) 2 times; (ch 2, 4 dc in next ch-2 sp) 4 times, ch 2, sk 3 dc, dc in next dc, (ch 2, dc in next dc) 2 times; dc in top of turning ch; ch 3, turn.

Row 8: Sk first dc, dc in next dc, (ch 2, dc in next dc) 3 times, (ch 2, 4 dc in next sp) 3 times, ch 2, sk 3 dc, dc in next dc, (ch 2, dc in next dc) 3 times; dc in top of turning ch. Do not turn.

Begin row of scallops on side: Ch 6, sl st in top corner of Row 6, ch 6, sl st in top corner of Row 4, ch 6, sl st in top corner of Row 2; ch 1, turn.

(In next ch-6 lp work 11 sc) 2 times, in half of next lp work 6 sc; turn.

(Ch 6, sl st in center sc on next lp) 2 times, ch 1, turn.

Over first lp work 11 sc and over half of second lp work 6 sc; ch 6, turn.

Sl st in center sc on next lp, ch 1, turn.

Row 9: Over top lp work 11 sc, (5 sc in rem ch-sp on row below) 2 times, sl st in top of last dc of Row 8; * ch 3, dc in next dc, (ch 2, dc in next dc) 4 times, (ch 2, 4 dc in next sp) 2 times, ch 2, sk 3 dc, dc in next dc, (ch 2, dc in next dc) 4 times; dc in top of turning ch; ch 3, turn.

Row 10: Sk first dc, dc in next dc, (ch 2, dc in next dc) 5 times; ch 2, 4 dc in next sp, ch 2, sk 3 dc, dc in next dc, (ch 2, dc in next dc) 5 times, ch 3, sl st in top of ch-3 at beg of Row 9; ch 2, working along scalloped edge, dc in center sc of first 5-sc grp; ch 2, dc in first sc of next 5-sc grp, ch 2, dc in center sc of same 5-sc grp, ch 2, dc in first sc of next 11-sc grp, (ch 2, sk sc, dc in next sc) 5 times; ch 2, dc in center sc of next 5-sc grp, ch 2, dc in first sc of next 5-sc grp, ch 2, dc in center sc of same 5-sc grp; ch 2, dc in top corner of Row 1; ch 3, sl st in corner of border, ch 5, turn.

Row 11: Sl st in third ch from hook, ch 2, sk next ch-3 and ch-2 sp, dc in next sp, (ch 5, sl st in third ch from hook, ch 2, dc in next sp) 12 times; ch 3, sl st in top of ch-3. (*Note:* Work continues across top of edging.) Ch 3, dc in next dc, (ch 2, dc in next dc) 6 times, ch 2, sk 2 dc, dc in next dc, (ch 2, dc in next dc) 6 times; dc in top of turning ch; ch 3, turn.

Rows 12–21: Rep rows 2–11 for pattern for required length. At beg of Row 21, work sl st into ch-2 sp, ch 3, dc in top corner of Row 10, turn and continue Row 11.

FINISHING: With double strand of sewing thread, whipstitch border to outside edges of spread, gathering or pleating for fullness at corners. Sew ends of border together if border fits around all four sides. If border fits around three sides, finish the fourth side by working a row of dc across the top of the spread.

SPREADS AND AFGHANS

Arrowhead Afghan With Popcorn Stitches

Shown on page 58.

Afghan measures 44x58 inches.

MATERIALS
Columbia-Minerva Nantuck brushed acrylic knitting worsted yarn (1¾-ounce ball): 14 balls of pale yellow, 11 balls of off-white
Size F aluminum crochet hook

Abbreviations: See page 78.
Gauge: 4½ dc = 1 inch; 3 dc rows = 1 inch. One block measures 14 inches square.

INSTRUCTIONS
Note: The afghan shown is made of 12 blocks arranged in four rows, each row containing three blocks. You may make the afghan larger, if you like, by adding more blocks in multiples of three, for length, or four, for width. Two additional balls of yarn are required for each extra block.

YELLOW BLOCK (make 6): With off-white, ch 6; join with sl st to form ring.

Rnd 1: Ch 6, (trc in ring, ch 2) 11 times; join with sl st in fourth ch of beg ch-6—12 ch-2 sp.

Rnd 2: Sl st in next ch-2 sp; **ch 3, 4 dc in same sp, drop lp from hook, insert hook in top of ch-3 and pull dropped lp through— beg pc made;** (ch 4, **5 dc in next ch-2 sp, drop lp from hook, insert hook in top of first dc of the 5-dc grp and pull dropped lp through—pc made**) 11 times; ch 4, join with sl st in top of beg pc. Fasten off off-white.

Rnd 3: Join yellow in top of any pc; ch 8, * dc in next pc, (ch 2, sc in next ch-4 sp) 2 times; ch 2, dc in next pc, ch 5; rep from * around; end ch 2, join with sl st in third ch of beg ch-8.

Rnd 4: Ch 3, * in next ch-5 sp work **3 dc, ch 3, and 3 dc—corner made;** dc in next dc, (ch 2, dc in next sc) 2 times, ch 2, dc in next dc; rep from * around; end ch 2, sl st in top of ch-3 at beg of rnd.

Rnd 5: Ch 3, dc in next 3 dc, * ch 1, in ch-3 corner sp work dc, ch 3, and dc, ch 1, dc in 4 dc, (ch 2, dc in next dc) 3 times; dc in next 3 dc; rep from * around; end ch 2, join with sl st to top of ch-3 at beg of rnd.

Rnd 6: Ch 3, * dc in next 3 dc, dc in ch-1 sp, dc in next dc, in ch-3 corner sp work 2 dc, ch 3, and 2 dc; dc in next dc, dc in ch-1 sp, dc in next 4 dc, (ch 2, dc in next dc) 3 times; rep from * around; end ch 2, join with sl st in top of ch-3.

Rnd 7: Ch 3, * dc in next 7 dc, ch 1, in ch-3 corner sp work dc, ch 3, and dc, ch 1, dc in 8 dc, (ch 2, dc in next dc) 3 times; rep from * around; end ch 2, join with sl st in top of ch-3.

Rnd 8: Ch 3, * dc in next 7 dc, dc in ch-1 sp, dc in dc, in ch-3 corner sp work 2 dc, ch 3, and 2 dc; dc in dc, dc in ch-1 sp, dc in next 8 dc, (ch 2, dc in next dc) 3 times; rep from * around; end ch 2, join with sl st in top of ch-3.

Rnd 9: Ch 3, * dc in next 11 dc, ch 1, in ch-3 corner sp work dc, ch 3, and dc; ch 1, dc in next 12 dc, (ch 2, dc in next dc) 3 times; rep from * around; end ch 2, join with sl st in top of ch-3.

Rnd 10: Ch 5, sk 2 dc, dc in next dc, ch 2, sk 2 dc, dc in next dc, * dc in next 5 dc, dc in ch-1 sp, dc in dc; in ch-3 corner sp work 2 dc, ch 3, and 2 dc; dc in dc, dc in ch-1 sp, dc in 6 dc, (ch 2, sk 2 dc, dc in next dc) 2 times; (ch 2, dc in next dc) 3 times; (ch 2, sk 2 dc, dc in next dc) 2 times; rep from * around; end ch 2, join to third ch of beg ch-5.

Rnd 11: Ch 5, dc in next dc, ch 2, dc in next dc, * dc in next 9 dc, ch 2, in corner sp work dc, ch 3, and dc; ch 2, dc in next 10 dc, (ch 2, dc in next dc) 7 times; rep from * around; end ch 2, join to third ch of ch-5 at beg of rnd.

Rnd 12: Ch 5, dc in next dc, ch 2, dc in next dc, * dc in next 9 dc, ch 2, dc in next dc, ch 2; in ch-3 corner sp work dc, ch 3, and dc; (ch 2, dc in next dc) 2 times, dc in next 9 dc, (ch 2, dc in next dc) 3 times, pc in next ch-2 sp, dc in next dc, (ch 2, dc in next dc) 3 times; rep from * around; end ch 2, join to third ch of beg ch-5.

Rnd 13: Ch 5, dc in next dc, ch 2, dc in next dc, ch 2, sk 2 dc, dc in next dc, * dc in next 6 dc, (ch 2, dc in next dc) 2 times; ch 2, in ch-3 corner sp work dc, ch 3, and dc; (ch 2, dc in next dc) 3 times; dc in next 6 dc, ch 2, sk 2 dc, dc in next dc; (ch 2, dc in next dc) 2 times; (pc in next ch-2 sp, dc in next dc, ch 2, dc in next dc) 2 times; ch 2, dc in next dc, ch 2, sk 2 dc, dc in next dc; rep from * around; end with pc in last ch-2 sp, join with sl st to third ch of beg ch-5.

Rnd 14: Ch 3, pc in next ch-2 sp, dc in next dc, (ch 2, dc in next dc) 2 times; ch 2, sk 2 dc, dc in next dc; * dc in next 3 dc, (ch 2, dc in next dc) 3 times; ch 2, in ch-3 corner sp work dc, ch 3, and dc; (ch 2, dc in next dc) 4 times; dc in next 3 dc, ch 2, sk 2 dc, dc in next dc, (ch 2, dc in next dc) 2 times; (pc in next ch-2 sp, dc in next dc, ch 2, dc in next dc) 3 times; ch 2, dc in next dc, ch 2, sk 2 dc, dc in next dc; rep from * around; end with pc in last ch-2 sp, dc in dc, ch 2, join to top of ch-3.

Rnd 15: Ch 5, sk pc, dc in next dc, pc in next sp, dc in next dc, (ch 2, dc in next dc) 2 times; * ch 2, sk 2 dc, dc in next dc, (ch 2, dc in next dc) 4 times, ch 2, in corner sp work dc, ch 3, and dc; (ch 2, dc in next dc) 5 times, ch 2, sk 2 dc, dc in next dc, (ch 2, dc in next dc) 2 times; (pc in next ch-2 sp, dc in next dc, ch 2, dc in next dc) 4 times; ch 2, dc in next dc; rep from * around; end pc in last ch-2 sp, join to third ch of beg ch-5.

Rnd 16: Ch 3, (pc in next ch-2 sp, dc in next dc, ch 2, dc in next dc) 2 times; * (ch 2, dc in next dc) 6 times; 3 dc in corner sp; dc in next dc, (ch 2, dc in next dc) 7 times; (pc in next sp, dc in next dc, ch 2, dc in next dc) 5 times; rep from * around; end pc in last sp, dc in dc, ch 2, join to top of ch-3.

Rnd 17: Ch 5, dc in next dc, (pc in next sp, dc in next dc, ch 2, dc in next dc) 2 times; * (ch 2, dc in next dc) 4 times; 2 dc in next ch-2 sp, dc in next 2 dc, 3 dc in next dc, dc in next 2 dc, 2 dc in next ch-2 sp, dc in next dc, (ch 2, dc in next dc) 5 times; (pc in next sp, dc in next dc, ch 2, dc in next dc) 6 times; rep from * around; end pc in last sp, dc in dc, ch 2, join to third ch of beg ch-5.

Rnd 18: Ch 1, sc in same st as join, (2 sc in next sp, sc in dc, sc in pc, sc in dc) 2 times; (2 sc in next sp, sc in next dc) 5 times, * sc in next 5 dc, 3 sc in corner dc, sc in next 6 dc, (2 sc in next sp, sc in next dc) 5 times, (sc in pc, sc in dc, 2 sc in sp, sc in dc) 6 times, (2 sc in next sp, sc in next dc) 4 times; rep from * around; join with sl st to first sc; fasten off.

OFF-WHITE BLOCK (make 6): Work same as the yellow block except make the following changes: Work rnds 1 and 2 with yellow. Work rnds 3–17 with off-white. Work Rnd 18 with yellow.

ASSEMBLY: With yellow yarn, whipstitch the six yellow and six white blocks together in four rows, each row with three blocks. Alternate the colors to create a checkerboard pattern.

BORDER: *Rnd 1:* With yellow yarn, sc in each sc around outside edges of afghan; in each corner st work 3 sc. Fasten off yellow.

Rnd 2: Join off-white in any corner st, ch 5, dc in same st, ch 2, dc in same st; * sk 2 sc, in next sc make **dc, ch 2, dc—V st made;** rep from * across side of afghan; sk last 1 or 2 sc before corner and in corner st work (dc, ch 2) 2 times and dc.

Note: An odd-number of V sts on each side is necessary to work Rnd 3 of the border. You may need to skip one sc between groups once or twice to adjust the spacing. The afghan shown has 95 V sts on each of the long sides and 71 V sts on each of the short sides.

Work rem sides and corners to correspond; join with sl st in third ch of beg ch-5. Fasten off.

Rnd 3: Join yellow in *first* ch-2 sp of any corner; ch 3, 2 dc in same sp, ch 3, sl st in top of last dc made, 2 dc in same place; * **in next ch-2 sp work 3 dc, ch 3, sl st in top of last dc made, and 2 dc—shell made;** dc in next ch-2 sp; rep from * across side of afghan; in both ch-2 sp of corner work shell; rep from first * to work next side. Work rem corners and sides to correspond; join with sl st in top of ch-3. Fasten off.

Hexagonal-Swirl Bedspread

Shown on pages 60 and 61.

Bedspread measures about 84 inches square.

MATERIALS
J. & P. Coats Knit-Cro-Sheen mercerized crochet cotton in desired color (400-yard ball): 1 ball makes 5 motifs
Size 7 steel crochet hook or size to obtain gauge
Sewing thread to match crochet cotton

Abbreviations: See page 78.
Gauge: Each individual motif measures about 5 inches across at the widest points.

INSTRUCTIONS
Note: The bedspread shown is an antique and is made from crochet cotton that is no longer available. To achieve an antique look, wash your assembled spread in *hot* water (add some bleach). Dry it in a machine dryer.

HEXAGON (make 347): Beg at center, ch 6, join with sl st to form ring.

Rnd 1: Ch 3, 2 dc in ring, (ch 2, 3 dc in ring) 5 times; ch 2, join with sl st in top of beg ch-3.

Rnd 2: Sl st into next dc, ch 3, dc in next dc; * in next ch-2 sp work 3 dc; ch 2, sk dc, dc in next 2 dc; rep from * around; end ch 2, join with sl st in top of beg ch-3.

Rnd 3: Sl st in next 2 dc, ch 3, dc in next 2 dc; * in next ch-2 sp work 4 dc; ch 3, sk 2 dc, dc in next 3 dc; rep from * around; end ch 3, join in top of ch-3.

Rnd 4: Sl st in next 2 dc, ch 3, dc in next 4 dc; * in ch-3 sp work 5 dc; ch 3, sk 2 dc, dc in next 5 dc; rep from * around; end ch-3, join in top of ch-3.

Rnd 5: Sl st in next 2 dc, ch 3, dc in 7 dc; * in ch-3 sp work 5 dc; ch 3, sk 2 dc, dc in next 8 dc; rep from * around; end ch 3, join in top of ch-3.

Rnd 6: Sl st in next 2 dc, ch 3, dc in 10 dc; * in ch-3 sp work 5 dc; ch 3, sk 2 dc, dc in next 11 dc; rep from * around; end ch 3, join in top of ch-3.

Rnd 7: Sl st in next 2 dc, ch 3, dc in 13 dc,; * in ch-3 sp work 5 dc; ch 3, sk 2 dc, dc in next 14 dc; rep from * around; end ch 3, join in top of ch-3.

Rnd 8: Sl st in next 2 dc, ch 3, dc in 16 dc; in ch-3 sp work 5 dc; ch 3, sk 2 dc, dc in next 17 dc; rep from * around; end ch 3, join in top of ch-3; fasten off.

ASSEMBLY: With double strand of matching color sewing thread, whipstitch two motifs together along edges of one dc section. (Do not sew the ch-3 lps together; these lps establish the points of the hexagon.) Sew 11 rows with 17 hexagons and 10 rows with 16 hexagons. With a 17-hexagon row on each end, sew rows together.

continued

BORDER: With the right side of spread facing, join thread in first dc of any 22-dc grp of any motif; ch 1, sc in same st.

Rnd 1: * Sk 2 dc, in next dc work **(dc, ch 2) 3 times, dc in same st—shell made;** sk 2 dc, sc in next dc; rep from * 2 times more; sk 2 dc, shell in last dc of grp; sc in first dc of next 22-dc grp. Rep from first * around; join with sl st to first sc.

Rnd 2: Sl st in next dc and into ch-2 sp, sc in same sp; * ch 4, sc in next ch-2 sp; rep from * around; end ch 4, join in first sc.

Rnd 3: Sl st in ch-4 sp, ch 3, 2 dc in same sp; * ch 3, 3 dc in next sp, ch 3, sc in next sp, ch 3, 3 dc in next sp; rep from * around; end ch 3, join in top of ch-3; fasten off.

Filet Bedspread And Pillow Cover

Shown on pages 62–63.

Bedspread measures 65 inches wide, plus the border on each side, and 77 inches long. The pillow cover measures 13 inches wide, plus the 8¼-inch border, and 77 inches long. Each bedspread panel measures 13 inches wide. The border is 8¼ inches at its widest point.

MATERIALS
Lily Sugar 'n' Cream baby and fashion crochet cotton (1.25-ounce skein): 75 skeins of white or ecru
Sewing thread to match crochet cotton
Size 3 steel crochet hook or size to obtain gauge

Abbreviations: See page 78.
Gauge: 6 dc = 1 inch; 3 rows = 1 inch.

INSTRUCTIONS
Note: The spread shown is an antique and is made from a coarse crochet cotton that is no longer available. The yarn listed in the materials list will produce a

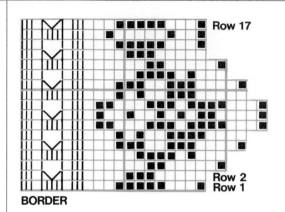

BORDER

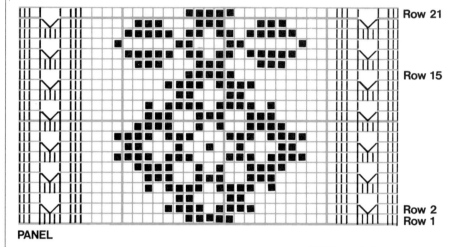

PANEL

- ■ **Block (bl)**
- □ **Space (sp)**
- ⦀ **3 dc block**
- ⋈ **Ch-3 loops over 5 dc**

bedspread of similar size.

For a smaller-gauge panel, use these instructions with Size 10 thread and Size 7 steel hook.

The panel construction of this spread allows you to adjust its length and width to fit any size bed. First, determine the amount of crocheting you can accomplish with the materials you choose to use, then purchase the amount of thread required for the size of the spread you want to make.

BEDSPREAD PANEL (make 5): Beg at bottom, ch 102.

Row 1: Dc in fourth ch from hook, dc in next ch, ch 1, sk ch, dc in next 5 ch; ch 1, sk ch, dc in next 3 ch; (ch 2, sk 2 ch, dc in next ch) 10 times, dc in next 15 ch, (ch 2, sk 2 ch, dc in next ch) 10 times; dc in next 2 ch, ch 1, sk ch, dc in next 5 ch, ch 1, sk ch, dc in last 3 ch; ch 3, turn.

Row 2: Sk first dc, dc in next 2 dc, ch 1, dc in next dc, ch 3, sc in center dc on 5-dc grp, ch 3, sk dc, dc in next dc, ch 1, dc in next 3 dc, (ch 2, dc in next dc) 8 times—8 sp; (2 dc in next ch-2 sp, dc in next dc) 2 times—2 bl; dc in next 6 dc—2 bl; ch 2, sk 2 dc, dc in next dc—1 sp; dc in next 6 dc—2 bl; (2 dc in next ch-2 sp, dc in next dc) 2 times; (ch 2, dc in next dc) 8 times—8 sp; dc in next 2 dc, ch 1, dc in next dc, ch 3, sc in center sc of 5-dc grp, ch 3, sk dc, dc in next dc, ch 1, dc in 2 dc and top of ch-3; ch 3, turn.

Row 3: Sk first dc, dc in next 2 dc, ch 1, dc in next dc, ch 5, dc in next dc, ch 1, dc in next 3 dc; (ch 2, dc in next dc) 8 times; ch 2, sk 2 dc, dc in next 7 dc, ch 2, sk 2 dc, dc in next dc, ch 2, dc in next dc, ch 2, sk 2 dc, dc in next 7 dc, ch 2, sk 2 dc, dc in next dc, (ch 2, dc in next dc) 8 times; dc in next 2 dc, ch 1, dc in next dc, ch 5, dc in next dc, ch 1, dc in next 2 dc and top of ch-3; ch 3, turn.

Row 4: Sk first dc, dc in next 2 dc, ch 1, dc in next dc, 5 dc in ch-5 lp, dc in next dc, ch 1, dc in next 3 dc; (ch 2, dc in next dc) 6 times, 2 dc in ch-2 sp, dc in next dc, (ch 2, dc in next dc, 2 dc in ch-2 sp, dc in next 7 dc, 2 dc in ch-2 lp, dc in next dc) 2 times; ch 2, dc in next dc, 2 dc in ch-2 sp, dc in next dc, (ch 2, dc in next dc) 6 times, dc in next 2 dc, ch 1, dc in next dc, 5 dc in ch-5 lp, dc in next dc, ch 1, dc in 2 dc and top of ch-3; ch 3, turn.

Rows 5–21: Continue to work panel referring to chart, *opposite*. Read chart from left to right when working the odd-numbered rows and from right to left when working the even-numbered rows.

Work through Row 21, then repeat rows 2–21 ten times more. Rep rows 2–15 once. Continue to work the three-row pattern repeat on both sides as established. Fasten off.

BORDER (make 2): Ch 51.
Row 1: Dc in fourth ch from hook, dc in next 2 ch, (ch 2, sk 2 ch, dc in next ch) 3 times; dc in next 15 ch, (ch 2, sk 2 ch, dc in next ch) 3 times, dc in next 2 ch, ch 1, sk ch, dc in next 5 ch, ch 1, sk ch, dc in next 3 ch; ch 3, turn.

Row 2: Sk first dc, dc in next 2 dc, ch 1, dc in next dc, ch 3, sc in center dc of 5-dc grp, ch 3, sk dc, dc in next dc; ch 1, dc in next 3 dc; (ch 2, dc in next dc) 3 times, ch 2, sk 2 dc, dc in next 10 dc, ch 2, sk 2 dc, dc in next dc, (ch 2, dc in next dc) 3 times, ch 2, sk 2 dc, dc in top of turning ch; ch 8, turn.

Row 3: Dc in fourth, fifth, and sixth ch from hook, ch 2, dc in next dc, (ch 2, dc in next dc) 4 times, 2 dc in ch-2 sp, dc in next 4 dc, (ch 2, sk 2 dc, dc in next dc) 2 times; (ch 2, dc in next dc) 4 times, dc in next 2 dc, ch 1, dc in next dc, ch 5, dc in next dc, ch 1, dc in next 2 dc and top of ch-3; ch 3, turn.

Row 4: Sk first dc, dc in next 2 dc, ch 1, dc in next dc, 5 dc in ch-5 lp, dc in dc, ch 1, dc in next 3 dc; (ch 2, dc in next dc) 5 times, 2 dc in ch-2 lp, dc in next 7 dc, 2 dc in ch-2 lp, dc in next dc, ch 2, dc in next dc; 2 dc in ch-2 lp, dc in next dc; (ch 2, dc in next dc) 2 times, ch 2, sk 2 dc, dc in top of turning-ch; ch 8, turn.

Rows 5–8: Work from chart, *opposite*; at end of Row 8, ch 3, turn.

Rows 9–17: Work from chart, *opposite*, working turning ch-3 at end of each row.

Rep rows 2-17 for pattern until border length matches length of panel. *Note:* Continue to work the three-row pattern repeat at the sides as established. Fasten off.

ASSEMBLY: Using sewing thread, sew five panels together. Sew border to each side.

TOP AND BOTTOM FINISHING: With right side facing, join thread at bottom of border; work ch-3 lps and sc evenly spaced across the edge of the spread; fasten off.

Join thread in ch-3 lp at the outside edge of the first panel, * ch 3, sc in next lp; rep from * across to lp above the outside edge of the fifth panel; ch 3, turn. Work three more rows of ch-3 lps across the five panels; fasten off.

Rep these instructions along the opposite edge of the spread.

PILLOW COVER: Make one panel following the instructions for the Bedspread Panel. Work desired length. Then work one border to fit the length. Sew border to one side of panel.

Work one row of sc evenly spaced across the short sides of the cover to stabilize it.

Woven Afghan

Shown on page 65.

Afghan measures 51x65 inches.

MATERIALS
Bernat Berella "4" (100-gram ball): 13 balls of off-white; 1 ball *each* of blue and raspberry
Size J aluminum crochet hook

Abbreviations: See page 78.
Gauge: 7 hdc = 2 inches.

INSTRUCTIONS
With off-white, ch 228.
Row 1: Hdc in third ch from hook and in each ch across—227 hdc, counting turning ch as st; ch 2, turn.

Row 2: Working in back lp, sk first hdc, hdc in each st across; end with hdc in top of turning ch; ch 2, turn.

Rows 3–4: Rep Row 2; end Row 4 with ch 3, turn.

Note: The next two rows form an open-weave pattern that establishes the warp for weaving the colored strands after the crocheting is completed.

Row 5: Working in front lps, * sk hdc, sc in next hdc, ch 3; rep from * across; end sc in top of turning ch—114 ch-3 lps; ch 3, turn.

Row 6: Hdc in first ch-3 lp, ch 1; * hdc in next ch-3 lp, ch 1; rep from * across row; end hdc in last ch-3 lp—114 hdc; ch 2, turn.

Row 7: Working in front lps, sk first hdc, hdc in each ch and hdc across; end hdc in top of turning ch-3 lp; ch 2, turn.

Row 8: Rep Row 2; ch 3, turn.

Row 9: **Sk first hdc, yo, draw up lp in next hdc, sk next hdc, yo, draw up lp in next hdc, yo, draw through all 5 lps on hook— beg star made; ch 1 for eye; * yo, draw up lp in last hdc worked in, yo, sk hdc, draw up lp in next hdc, yo, draw through all 5 lps on hook, ch 1 for eye—star made;** rep from * across row; end hdc in top of turning ch—113 stars; ch 3, turn.

continued

Row 10: Yo, draw up lp in first eye, yo, draw up lp in next eye, yo, draw through 5 lps on hook, ch 1 for eye; * yo, draw up lp in eye just made, yo, draw up lp in next eye, yo, draw through 5 lps on hook; rep from * across row; end yo, draw up lp in eye just made, yo, draw up lp in top of turning ch, yo, draw through 5 lps on hook, ch 1 for eye—113 stars; ch 2, turn.

Row 11: Hdc in each eye and star across, hdc in top of turning ch—228 hdc; ch 2, turn.

Rows 12–17: Rep rows 4–9.

Rows 18–24: Rep Row 10; end rows 18–23 with ch 3, turn; end Row 24 with ch 2, turn.

Row 25: Rep Row 11.

Rows 26–38: Rep rows 4–16; end Row 38 with ch 2, turn.

Rows 39–52: Rep rows 3–16.

Row 53: Rep Row 9.

Rows 54–68: Rep Row 10; end rows 54–67 with ch 3, turn; end Row 68 with ch 2, turn.

Row 69: Rep Row 11.

Rows 70–82: Rep rows 4–16.

Rows 83–118: Rep rows 3–38.

Rows 119–120: Rep Row 2; do not fasten off or turn work.

EDGING (on long sides only): Working from left to right (reverse sc), * ch 1, sk 1 st, sc in next st; rep from * across to opposite corner; fasten off.

With wrong side facing, join off-white to left end of foundation ch and work same as opposite side; fasten off.

FINISHING: Cut 368 off-white 14-inch-long yarn strands. Holding four strands tog in one bundle, fold the strands in half and loop the ends through the edges bet every other row to make the fringe on the short sides of the afghan. Do not attach fringe to ends of the open-weave rows (rows 5–6).

Cut forty-eight 82-inch-long strands of blue yarn and twenty-four 82-inch-long strands of raspberry yarn. Holding three blue strands together, weave the combined strands through the first four open-weave rows (under and over the ch-3 lps and over and under the hdc and ch-1 sp). Tie the ends of the strands together in an overhand knot at each end of the afghan. Weave the raspberry strands in the next four open-weave rows. Weave the blue strands in the last four open-weave rows. Rep the weaving on the opposite side of the afghan to mirror the first side. Trim the fringe even.

Diamond-Bobble Afghan

Shown on page 64.

Afghan measures 50x62 inches.

MATERIALS
Lion Brand Sayelle (3.5-ounce skein): 22 skeins of eggshell (No. 99)
Size G crochet hook or size to obtain gauge
Tapestry needle

Abbreviations: See page 78.
Gauge: Motif measures 6 inches square.

INSTRUCTIONS
Note: The symbol ** in these instructions indicates where the last repeat in the row ends. The symbol does not designate pattern repeats within the rounds.

MOTIF (make 80): Ch 8, join with sl st to form ring.

Rnd 1: Ch 5, (in ring work hdc, dc, trc, dc, hdc, and ch 3) 3 times; end hdc, dc, trc, dc, join with sl st in second ch of beg ch-5.

Rnd 2: Ch 6, in first ch-3 lp **(yo, draw up lp to ½ inch) 4 times, yo, draw through 8 lps, yo, draw through 2 lps—bobble made;** ch 3, dc in same ch-3 lp, * ch 2, dc around post of next trc, ch 2, in next ch-3 lp work dc, ch 3, bobble, ch 3, and dc; rep from * 2 times more; end ch 2, dc around post of next trc, ch 2; join with sl st in third ch of beg ch-6.

Rnd 3: Ch 3, work bobble around post of turning-ch just below the same st as join; in next ch-3 lp work 4 dc; dc in top of bobble, 4 dc in next ch-3 lp; * bobble around post of next dc, (ch 2, bobble around post of next dc) 2 times; in next ch-3 lp work 4 dc; dc in top of bobble, 4 dc in next ch-3 lp; rep from * 2 times more; end (bobble around post of next dc, ch 2) 2 times; join with sl st in top of beg bobble.

Rnd 4: Ch 1, sc in next 4 dc; in next dc work dc, ch 2, and dc; sc in next 4 dc; * sk bobble; in next bobble work dc, ch 2, and dc; sk bobble, sc in next 4 dc; in next dc work **dc, ch 2, and dc—corner made;** sc in next 4 dc; rep from * 2 times more; end sk bobble, in next bobble work dc, ch 2, and dc; join with sl st in first sc.

Rnd 5: Ch 3, dc in next 3 sc; * ch 3, bobble in ch-2 corner sp, ch 3; sk dc, dc in next 4 sc, ch 2, bobble in next ch-2 sp, ch 2; sk dc **, dc in next 4 sc; rep from * 2 times more; rep from * to **; join with sl st in top of beg ch-3.

Rnd 6: Ch 3, dc in next 3 dc, * in ch-3 lp work 5 dc; ch 3 for corner; in next ch-3 lp work 5 dc; dc in next 4 dc, ch 2, dc in top of next bobble, ch 2 **, dc in 4 dc; rep from * 2 times; rep from * to **; join with sl st in top of beg ch-3; fasten off.

FINISHING: Arrange motifs in 10 rows of eight motifs each. Thread tapestry needle with single strand of yarn. Sew motifs tog through back lps of last rnd.

BORDER: *Rnd 1:* Join thread in any ch-3 corner lp; ch 4, dc in same lp; * dc in next 9 dc, 2 dc in ch-2 sp, dc in next dc, 2 dc in ch-2 sp, dc in next 9 dc, dc in corner lp, 2 dc in join of 2 blocks, dc in corner lp of next block; rep from * along side to corner; in corner lp work dc, ch 1, and dc; rep from first * to complete next side; work rem two sides to correspond; join with sl st to third ch of beg ch-4.

Rnd 2: Ch 3, * 3 dc in ch-1 corner sp; dc in each dc to next ch-1 corner sp; rep from * around; join with sl st to top of ch-3 at beg of rnd; fasten off.

Lavender and Lace Afghan

Shown on page 66.

Afghan measures 48x59 inches including border.

MATERIALS
Lion Brand Debyshire 3-ply baby and sport yarn (2-ounce skein): 9 skeins of white, 6 skeins of lavender
Size F aluminum crochet hook

Abbreviations: See page 78.
Gauge: 11 dc = 2 inches; 4 dc rows = 2 inches. Block measures 11 inches square.

INSTRUCTIONS
BLOCK (make 20): With lavender, starting at center, ch 8; join with sl st to form ring.

Rnd 1: Ch 4, (dc in ring, ch 1) 11 times; join with sl st in third ch of beg ch-4.

Rnd 2: **Ch 3, 4 dc in same st as join, drop lp from hook, insert hook in top of beg ch-3, pull the dropped lp through—beg pc made;** ch 3, **5 dc in next dc, drop lp from hook, insert hook in top of first dc of the 5-dc grp and pull the dropped lp through—pc made;** ch 3, (pc in next dc, ch 3) 10 times; join last ch-3 with sl st in top of beg pc—12 pc.

Rnd 3: Ch 3, 3 dc in next ch-3 sp, * dc in next pc, 3 dc in next ch-3 sp; rep from * around; join with sl st in top of ch-3 at beg of rnd—48 dc.

Rnd 4: Ch 5, dc in same st as join; * ch 1, sk 2 dc; in next dc work dc, ch 2, and dc; rep from * around; end ch 1, sl st in third ch of beg ch-5.

Rnd 5: Ch 5, * dc in next dc, ch 2; rep from * around; join last ch-2 with sl st to third ch of beg ch-5.

Rnd 6: Ch 3, * 2 dc in next ch-2 sp, dc in next dc; rep from * around; join with sl st to top of beg ch-3—96 dc.

Rnd 7: Ch 5, * sk dc, dc in next dc, ch 2; rep from * around; join last ch-2 with sl st to third ch of beg ch-5.

Rnd 8: Rep Rnd 5.

Rnd 9: Ch 6, * dc in next dc, ch 3, rep from * around; join last ch-3 with sl st to third ch of beg ch-6. Fasten off lavender.

Rnd 10: Join white with sl st in any ch-3 sp; ch 3, in same sp work 2 dc; * 3 dc in next ch-3 sp; rep from * around; join to top of ch-3 at beg of rnd.

Rnd 11: Ch 3; * pc in next dc, ch 1 tightly; (dc in next 2 dc, pc in next dc, ch 1 tightly) 6 times; dc in next dc, (ch 6, sc in center dc of next 3-dc grp) 5 times; ch 6, dc in first dc of next 3-dc grp; rep from * around; end ch 3, dc in top of beg ch-3.

Rnd 12: Ch 1, 3 sc in lp just made, * sc in *each* dc and *each* pc along side of block; 3 sc in next ch-lp; (ch 6, sc in next ch-lp) 4 times; ch 6, 3 sc in next lp; rep from * around; end ch 3, dc in sc at beg of rnd.

Rnd 13: Ch 1, 3 sc in lp just made; * sc in each sc along side of block; 3 sc in next ch-lp; (ch 6, sc in next lp) 3 times; ch 6, 3 sc in next lp; rep from * around; end ch 3, dc in sc at beg of rnd.

Rnd 14: Ch 1, 3 sc in lp just made; * sc in each sc along side of block; 3 sc in next ch-lp; (ch 6, sc in next lp) 2 times; ch 6, 3 sc in next lp; rep from * around; end ch 3, dc in sc at beg of rnd.

Rnd 15: Ch 1, 3 sc in lp just made; * sc in each sc along side of block; 3 sc in next ch-lp; ch 6, sc in next lp, ch 6, 3 sc in next lp; rep from * around; end ch 3, dc in sc at beg of rnd.

Rnd 16: Ch 1, 3 sc in lp just made; * sc in each sc, 3 sc in next ch-lp, ch 6, 3 sc in next lp; rep from * around; end ch 6, sl st in sc at beg of rnd.

Rnd 17: Ch 1, * sc in *each* sc along side of block, 7 sc in corner lp; rep from * around; join with sl st in sc at beg of rnd. Fasten off.

Rnd 18: Join lavender with sc in any sc; sc in *each* sc around; join with sl st in sc at beg of rnd. Fasten off.

ASSEMBLY: With lavender yarn, sew through matching top lps to sew blocks together. Sew four blocks across for the width and five blocks down for the length.

BORDER: *Note:* After all blocks are finished and joined there will be 59 sts across the sides of each square.

Rnd 1: Join lavender yarn in any corner sc, in same st work 3 sc; sc in next 56 sts; * hdc in last 2 sc on side of block, hdc in joining bet blocks, hdc in first 2 sc on next block, sc in next 55 sc; rep from * across side of afghan, working 56 sc across last block and working 3 sc in next corner sc. Work rem three sides to correspond; join with sl st in first sc. Fasten off.

Rnd 2: Join white with sl st in any corner sc, ch 4, dc in same sc, ch 1, dc in next sc; * ch 1, sk sc, dc in next sc; rep from * across side of afghan up to the st before corner st, ch 1; in corner sc work dc, ch 1, and dc; ch 1, dc in next sc; rep from * around; end ch 1, join with sl st in third ch of beg ch-4.

Rnd 3: Sl st into corner sp, ch 3, 2 dc in same sp; (ch 2, 2 dc in next sp) 2 times; * ch 2, sk ch-1 sp, 2 dc in next ch-1 sp; rep from * across side of afghan up to first sp before corner; ch 2, 2 dc in next sp, ch 2, 3 dc in corner sp; (ch 2, 2 dc in next sp) 2 times; rep from first * to complete next side. Work rem two sides to correspond; end with ch 2, join with sl st in top of ch-3 at beg of rnd. Fasten off.

Rnd 4: Join lavender with sl st in center dc of any corner, ch 4, dc in same st as join; * ch 1, in next ch-2 sp work **dc, ch 1, and dc— shell made;** rep from * across side of afghan; ch 1, in center dc of corner work dc, ch 1, and dc; rep from first * to complete next side.

Work rem two sides to correspond; end with ch 1, join in third ch of beg ch-4. Fasten off.

Rnd 5: Join white with sl st in any ch-1 corner sp, ch 8, dc in same sp; ch 3, sc in next ch-1 sp; * ch 4, sc in ch-1 sp of next shell, ch 3; in ch-1 sp of next shell work dc, ch 4, and dc; ch 3, sc in ch-1 sp of next shell; rep from * across side of afghan up to last ch-1 sp before corner, ch 4, sc in ch-1 sp, ch 3; in ch-1 corner shell sp work dc, ch 5, and dc; ch 3, sc in ch-1 sp of next *continued* shell; rep from first * to complete next side. Work rem two sides to correspond; end with ch 3, join with sl st in third ch of beg ch-8.

Rnd 6: Sl st into corner ch-5 sp; ch 6, sl st in third ch from hook; dc in same sp, (ch 3, sl st in top of dc just made, dc in same sp) 10 times; ch 1, sc in next ch-4 sp. * Ch 3, dc in next ch-4 sp, (ch 3, sl st in top of dc just made, dc in same sp) 8 times, ch 3, sc in next ch-4 sp; rep from * across side of afghan up to next corner sp, ch 1; in corner sp work (dc, ch 3, sl st in top of dc just made) 11 times; dc in same sp; ch 1, sc in next ch-4 sp; rep from first * to complete next side. Work rem two sides to correspond; end with ch 1, sl st in third ch of beg ch-6. Fasten off.

Lacy Pillow Tops

Shown on page 67.

Finished crocheted pillow top measures 16½ inches square.

MATERIALS
DMC Splendida 2 cotton yarn (50-gram ball): for solid-colored top, 3 balls of white; for two-colored top, 1 ball of color A for center of block and 2 balls of color B for outside areas of block
Size F aluminum crochet hook
½ yard of fabric for pillow form
2 yards of ¼-inch-wide satin ribbon
Polyester fiberfill

Abbreviations: See page 78.
Gauge: 10 dc = 2 inches; 5 dc rows = 2 inches.

INSTRUCTIONS
Follow directions, *below,* to work the solid-colored pillow top, except do not change colors as noted. Always sl st to the starting point (the corner) to begin the next round.

For the two-colored pillow top, with color A, work rnds 1–9 of the afghan Block on page 75. Fasten off. With color B, work rnds 10–17. Fasten off.

Rnd 18: Join color A in center sc of any 7-sc corner-grp, in same st work 3 sc; * sc in 62 sc along side, in center st of next corner work 3 sc; rep from * around to complete rem three sides; join with sl st in first sc.

Rnd 19: * In corner sc work 3 sc, sc in each sc along side; rep from * 3 times more; join with sl st in first sc. Fasten off color A.

Rnd 20: In center sc of any corner join color B, ch 5, dc in same st, ch 1, dc in next sc; * (ch 1, sk sc, dc in next sc) 30 times, ch 1; in corner sc work dc, ch 2, and dc; ch 1, dc in next sc; rep from * around; end with ch 1, join with sl st in third ch of beg ch-5—32 sp along each side, plus 4 corner sp.

Rnd 21: Sl st to corner sp, ch 3, 2 dc in same sp; * (ch 2, 2 dc in next dc) 2 times; (ch 2, sk dc, 2 dc in next dc) 15 times; ch 2, 2 dc in next dc, ch 2, 3 dc in corner sp; rep from * around; end with 2 dc in top of same ch-3 used to join previous rnd, ch 2, sl st in top of ch-3 at beg of rnd. Fasten off B.

Rnd 22: In center dc of corner-grp join color A, ch 4, dc in same st; * (ch 1, in next ch-2 sp work **dc, ch 1, and dc—shell made**) 19 times; ch 1, shell in center dc of corner-grp; rep from * around; end with ch 1, sl st in third ch of beg ch-4. Fasten off color A.

Rnd 23: Join color B in ch-1 sp of any corner shell, ch 7, dc in same sp, ch 3, sc in next ch-1 sp; * (ch 3, in sp of next shell work **dc, ch 4, and dc—large shell made;** ch 3, sc in ch-1 sp of next shell, ch 4, sc in ch-1 sp of next shell) 6 times; (ch 3, in sp of next shell work dc, ch 4, and dc; ch 3, sc in next ch-1 sp) 2 times; rep from * around; end with ch 3, sl st in third ch of beg ch-7.

Rnd 24: Sl st to center of ch-4 corner sp, ch 1, sc in same sp; * ch 3, dc in ch-4 sp of large shell, (ch 3, sl st in dc just made, dc in same sp) 8 times; ch 3, sk ch-3 lp, sc in next ch-4 sp; rep from * around; end with ch 3, sl st in first sc at beg of rnd. Fasten off.

FINISHING: Cut two 13-inch squares from fabric for pillow top and back. With right sides facing, sew front to back; leave opening for turning. Clip corners, turn, and stuff with fiberfill. Sew opening closed. Pin, then baste the crocheted top to the pillow top, matching Rnd 19 of the crocheted piece with the edges of the fabric pillow. Use matching sewing thread to hand-sew the crocheted top to the stuffed pillow. Weave the satin ribbon through the dc of Rnd 20. Begin weaving in one corner and continue around pillow top. Tie ribbon ends in a bow to complete.

How to Care For Handmade Lace

To preserve the beauty of your handmade crocheted lace, treat it with the same care you would lavish on heirloom lace in your linen closet.

Repair all damaged lace before washing it. When sewing, insert the needle *between* threads rather than into them.

Holes are best repaired by duplicating the crochet stitches that make up the pattern. Experiment with hook sizes and threads before you actually repair the piece. To work the crochet patch that will fill the hole, start at the stitches below the hole. Then crochet the patch and hand-sew its top to the stitches at the top of the hole. Tack the sides, if necessary.

To remove stains, use a gentle bleach, such as lemon juice mixed with water. Or, use hydrogen peroxide, diluting it according to the manufacturer's directions.

Store your lace in a cool, dry place. Lay small pieces flat, without folding, between sheets of acid-free tissue paper. Loosely roll larger pieces around cardboard or wooden cylinders that have been wrapped with tissue paper. Wrap another piece of tissue paper around the outside of the lace.

CROCHETING PRIMER

To make your crocheting as pleasurable as possible, use these helpful tips when working the projects in this book.

Reading instructions

Following the instructions may seem difficult at first if you are a novice at crochet. Crocheting is worked in steps that are called rows or rounds. Within these rows or rounds, step sequences are set off by punctuation. Pay attention to commas, semicolons and periods.

Instructions also are written in an abbreviated form. Familiarize yourself with these abbreviations before beginning a project so you can quickly read the instructions. See the list on page 78 for the abbreviations that apply to projects in this book as well as other published crochet instructions.

Symbols are used to shorten directions and to indicate that a part of a pattern is repeated. An asterisk (*) indicates that there is a pattern repeat within a row or a round. Asterisks are used in groups of two, one appearing earlier in the row or round than the other. Work the stitches *between* the asterisks, then *repeat* the pattern between the asterisks as many times as indicated. For example, if the instructions read *ch 2, sk sc, dc in next 5 dc; rep from * 6 times more,* you will actually work the stitches between the asterisks a total of seven times.

A double asterisk (**) is used in this book to designate where the last pattern of a repeat ends within a set of instructions. For example, if the instructions read *ch 3, sk dc, dc in next 4 sc, ch 2 **, dc in next 4 dc; rep from * 2 times more; rep from * to **; join with sl st to top of ch-3,* you should work the stitches between the single asterisks a total of three times. Then repeat the instructions from the first * again but only up to the first **. Skip the remaining instructions between the *s. Work the directions that follow the *s to complete the round or row.

Parentheses also indicate repetition. Repeat the set of instructions within the parentheses the total number of times indicated before beginning the next step.

Working in rows

As you complete each row of stitching, you must turn your work over to begin the next row. Notice that you will always be working on the *wrong* side of the stitches of the previous row. Also notice the tiny holes at the tops of the previous row's stitches. Insert the hook into these holes so that each stitch in the row you are now working lies to the *left* of each stitch in the previous row.

At the end of each row you will work a "turning chain." Turning chains raise the level of your work along the edge to equal the height of the next row's stitches. Work the required number of chains, then turn the work over to begin the next row.

With the exception of the single crochet, all turning chains count as the first stitch of the next row. The following are guidelines for establishing the number of chains when working a straight-edged piece.

To begin a row of single crochet, chain 1, turn, and work the first single crochet in the first stitch of the row. For a row of half double crochet, chain 2, turn, and work the first half double crochet in the second stitch of the row. To begin a row of double crochet, chain 3, turn, and work the first double crochet in the second stitch of the row. For a row of treble crochet, chain 4, turn, and work the first treble crochet in the second stitch of the row.

The last stitch of each row is worked into the top stitch of the turning chain, except for single crochet stitches. Always crochet into two loops of the chain to avoid making a hole in your work.

Working in the foundation chain

Begin the first row of a pattern by working the first stitch in the appropriate chain. When starting a row of single crochet after completing this foundation chain,

work the first single crochet in the *second* chain from the hook; work a half double crochet in the *third* chain, a double crochet in the *fourth* chain, and a treble crochet in the *fifth* chain. Except when a row begins with a single crochet, count the group of chains at the beginning of a row as the first stitch of the row.

Working in rounds

Unlike patterns crocheted back and forth in rows, motifs such as circles, hexagons, some squares, and other medallion shapes are stitched in rounds that usually begin in the centers of the motifs. When you have crocheted completely around the shape, you have completed one round.

In most instances, you work with the right side facing you; the stitches are always on the right side of the work. As you crochet each stitch, insert the hook into the hole to the *right* of the stitch in the round below, rather than to the left as you do when working rows.

The instructions specifically cite the stitches needed to keep the work lying flat. As the motif increases in size, so will the number of stitches in each round.

Most rounds are joined with a slip stitch into the top chain of the beginning chain (first stitch). Work this slip stitch into two loops of the chain.

Keeping tension even

To keep stitches even and uniform in size, crochet over the *shank* of the hook. You will have better control over your stitching if you keep the thumb and middle finger of your left hand (if you're a right-handed crocheter) close to the area where you are stitching. A left-handed crocheter should use the thumb and middle finger of the right hand. To avoid stitching too tightly, draw up the loop in the stitch you are making and allow this loop to be almost twice as large as the loop already on the hook. If you do this, your work will remain soft and flexible rather than getting stiff.

continued

CROCHETING PRIMER

Abbreviations and Stitch Diagrams

Abbreviations

beg .... begin(ning)
bet .... between
bl .... block
ch .... chain
cl .... cluster
cont .... continue
dc .... double crochet
dec .... decrease
dtr .... double treble crochet
grp .... group
hdc .... half double crochet
inc .... increase
lp(s) .... loop(s)
pat .... pattern
pc .... popcorn
rem .... remaining
rep .... repeat
rnd .... round
sc .... single crochet
sk .... skip
sl st .... slip stitch
sp .... space
st(s) .... stitch(es)
tog .... together
trc .... treble crochet
yo .... yarn over
* .... repeat from * as indicated
( ) .... repeat between ( )s
as indicated

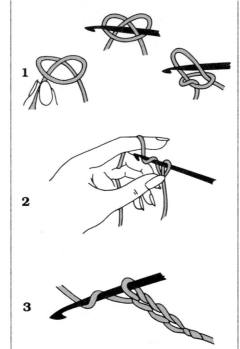

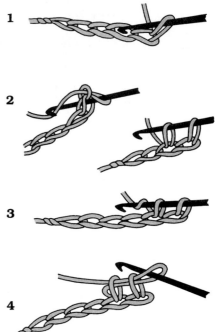

Chain Stitch

1 Start by making a slipknot on the hook about 6 inches from the yarn end. Pull one end of the yarn to tighten the knot.

2 Wrap yarn around the little finger of your left hand, and bring it up behind the next finger, under the middle finger, and back over the index finger. Hold the slipknot between your left thumb and middle finger. Hold the crochet hook between the right index finger and thumb, as you would a pencil.

3 Make a chain by wrapping the yarn over the hook and drawing it through the loop on the hook. Repeat Step 3 to make any number of chains.

Single Crochet

Chain 20.

1 Insert the crochet hook into the second chain from the hook, under the two upper strands of the stitch.

2 Wrap yarn over the hook and draw yarn through the chain—two loops are on the hook.

3 Wrap yarn over the hook.

4 Draw the yarn through the two loops on the hook—one single crochet made. Repeat steps 1–4 across the row of chains, working a single crochet in the *next* chain and in *each* chain across.

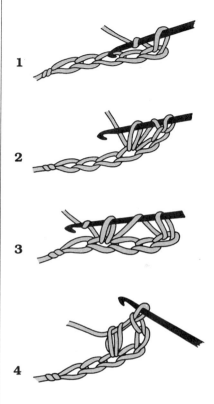

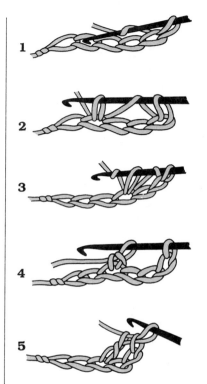

Half Double Crochet

Chain 20.
1 Wrap yarn over hook; insert hook into the third chain from the hook, under the two upper strands of the stitch.
2 Wrap yarn over the hook and draw a loop through the chain—three loops are on the hook.
3 Wrap yarn over the hook.
4 Draw yarn through the three loops on the hook—half double crochet made. Repeat steps 1–4 across the row, working a half double crochet in the *next* chain and in *each* chain across.

Double Crochet

Chain 20.
1 Wrap yarn over the hook; insert the hook into the fourth chain from the hook, under the two upper strands of the chain.
2 Wrap yarn over the hook and draw a loop through the chain—three loops are on the hook.
3 Wrap yarn over the hook.
4 Draw yarn through the first two loops on the hook—two loops remain on the hook.
5 Wrap yarn over the hook; draw the yarn through the last two loops on the hook—double crochet made. Repeat steps 1–5 across the row, working a double crochet in the *next* chain and in *each* chain across.

Slip Stitch

Chain 20.
1 Insert the crochet hook under the two top strands of the second chain from the hook. Wrap yarn over the hook, and, with a single motion, pull the yarn through the chain and the loop on the hook—slip stitch made. Insert the hook under the two top strands of the next chain; wrap yarn over the hook; draw the yarn through the chain and the loop on the hook.
2 Repeat Step 1, working a slip stitch in each chain across.

The slip stitch is used as a joining stitch when crocheting in rounds, or to bind and strengthen edges.

Treble Crochet

Chain 20.
1 Wrap yarn over hook two times; insert the hook into the fifth chain from the hook, under the two top strands of the chain.
2 Wrap yarn over hook and draw a loop through the chain—four loops are on the hook.
3 Wrap yarn over the hook and draw the yarn through the first two loops on the hook—three loops remain on hook.
4 Wrap yarn over the hook and draw the yarn through the next two loops on the hook—two loops remain on the hook.
5 Wrap yarn over the hook and draw the yarn through the remaining two loops on the hook—treble crochet made. Repeat steps 1–5, working treble crochet in *next* chain and *each* chain across.

ACKNOWLEDGMENTS

We would like to extend our special thanks to the following designers who contributed projects to this book. When more than one project appears on a page, the acknowledgment specifically cites the project with the page number. A page number alone indicates one designer contributed all of the projects listed on that page.

Mary Becker—64

Judith Brandeau—46–47

Dixie Falls—5, sampler; 40–41

Gail Kinkead—58, afghan; 66–67

Martha Koehler—22–23

Joyce Nordstrom—65

Sara Jane Treinen—4, flowers

A special thank-you to the following people, whose technical skills are greatly appreciated.

Betty Crist

Marie Holmstrand

Gail Kinkead

Peggy Leonardo

Margaret Sindelar

For their cooperation and courtesy, we extend a special thanks to the following sources for designs and projects, and for assistance in writing instructions.

Coats & Clark Inc.—6–7; 9–11; 42–43; 44–45
Dept. CS
P.O. Box 1010
Toccoa, GA 30577

Columbia-Minerva
P.O. Box 1240
Bessemer City, NC 28016

Lily Craft Products—24–25; 62–63
B. Blumenthal and Co., Inc.
140 Kero Rd.
Carlstadt, NJ 07072

We also are pleased to acknowledge the photographers whose talents and technical skills contributed much to this book.

Sean Fitzgerald—9; 24–25; 58–59; 60–61; 62–63

Hopkins Associates—4–5; 8; 22–23; 26–27; 28–29; 30–31; 64–65; 66–67

Mike Jensen—6–7; 10–11

Scott Little—40–41; 42–43; 44–45; 46–47

Have BETTER HOMES
AND GARDENS® magazine
delivered to your door.
For information, write to:
MR. ROBERT AUSTIN
P.O. BOX 4536
DES MOINES, IA 50336